CHINESE
FUNCTIONAL FOOD

Dang Yi, Peng Yong, Li Wenkui

NEW WORLD PRESS

First Edition 1999

Edited by Ren Lingjuan

Book Design by Fang Wei

Cover Design by He Yuting

ISBN-7-80005-555-8/G • 188

Published by
NEW WORLD PRESS
24 Baiwanzhuang Road, Beijing 100037, China

Distributed by
CHINA INTERNATIONAL BOOK TRADING
CORPORATION
35 Chegongzhuang Xilu, Beijing 100044, China
P. O. Box 399, Beijing, China

Printed in the People' s Republic of China

CONTENTS

Acknowledgements

To publish a book on Chinese functional food in English has been one of my goals for years. At the Beijing University of Chinese Medicine and Pharmacology (BUCMP), I have taught classes on and conducted research for 20 years in the field of traditional Chinese medicine. Since 1985, my main research has been maintaining health and rehabilitation with traditional Chinese medicine, particularly food therapy. In the past 10 years or so, I have taught classes for overseas students at BUCMP and the Academy of Chinese Medicine. One of major difficulties for overseas students learning about Chinese medicine and functional food is the lack of books written in English. I wrote this book to share what I have learnt in the past 20 years with those who want to understand Chinese medicine and functional food but need reference books written in English.

This study would be impossible without the personal encouragement of so many good people to whom I owe my hearty thanks.

Many people helped and encouraged me throughout the process of publishing this book, particularly my colleagues at the BUCMP, the Institute for the Advancement of Chinese Medicine (IACM) of Hong Kong Baptist University, and the Institute of Medicinal Plants at the Chinese Academy of Medical Sciences.

I thank Professor Drazigost Pokorn, the president of Institute of Hygiene, Medical Faculty, University of Ljubliana, Slovenia, Professors

i

Shaochia Chou and Furusawa of the Department of Pharmacology, John A. Burns School of Medicine, University of Hawaii, USA, Professor Cherl-Ho Lee from the Department of Food Technology, College of Natural Resources, Korea University, Professor Woo Kyung Ja from the Department of Food & Nutrition, College of Home Economics, Inha University, Inchon, and the President of the East Asian Society of Dietary Life in Korea, for inviting me to go abroad and stay at their institutes as a visiting scholar. This enabled me to collect more information about functional food in different countries. Some material of this book is based on the papers I produced at their institutes.

My special thanks to my Ph.D supervisors, Professor Xiao Peigen, member, Chinese Academy of Engineering Division, Medicine & Health Engineering, Professor Yeung Hinwing, director of Institute for the Advancement of Chinese Medicine (IACM), Hong Kong Baptist University and Professor Wang Liwei, Professor at Institute of Medicinal Plants, Chinese Academy of Medical Sciences and my Medical Science Master supervisor, Professor Weng Weijian, for his enlightened advice.

In revising this book to its present form I also received generous support from Mr. Leung Siuwai and Dr. Leung Heiwun, Yeung Hinwing and Xiao Peigen. I am grateful to them for their comments on the first draft of this book and their many kindnesses.

My special thanks to Professor Xiao Peigen for writing a foreword and recommending this book to the public.

In addition, I am most appreciative of my two co-authors, Mr. Peng Yong and Dr. Li Wenkui, for their collaboration in writing this book.

My special love and thanks to my husband, Mr. Wang Jianguo, whose encouragement has helped me in past studies and in writing this book. Despite the fact that there are many contributors, any errors of fact or supposition in this study remain, of course, my responsibility alone.

Dang Yi
July 25, 1998
Hong Kong

Foreword

Functional food is one of the hot issues in medical field. In the 21st century, "Human has to be back to the nature" will be more popularly echoed in our conduct. With the great improvement of the living standards, functional food (or healthy food) will doubtlessly draw much attention to our scientific studies.

In one of our previous articles entitled "Immunological aspects of Chinese medicinal plants as anti-aging drug" (J. Ethnopharm. 38: 167-175, 1993), we mentioned, "Interestingly, anti-aging agents have been integrated into diet as health foods in China since ancient times, such as walnut, black sesame, flax seed, Job's tears, euryale, lotus seed, apricot kernel, mulberry, hawthorn, Chinese date, sour jujube, longan aril, Chinese matrimonyvine fruit, kiwi, yam, garlic, lily bulbs, tea, chrysanthemum flower and several kinds of mushroom, including black ear mushroom, fragrant mushroom and silver ear mushroom, are still being popularly used as healthy food diets in China till present time. After the transition of the medical model towards prevention of diseases the prevalence of this trend will become move predominant."

In facing of the 21st century, such trend is indeed more and more distinctly standing out. It is needed, therefore, a book to introduce the knowledge of functional food in China.

Professor Dang Yi is a Chinese expert in combination of traditional Chinese medicine and Western medicine. She is well known in functional food research and excellent in explaining the principles of Chinese functional food in plain English. She has given numerous lectures on Chinese functional food in various countries, including the United States, Slovenia, Korea, etc. I am delighted to read her manuscripts of this book, which provides a good source of knowledge about Chinese functional food to Western scientists as well as laymen. I sincerely hope that the research and development of Chinese functional food will be further promoted through the endeavor of the people in the world. Their quality of life will be improved when they learn about using functional food in a proper way.

Prof. Xiao Peigen

Xiao Pei-Gen

Member, Chinese Academy of Engineering,
Division Medicine & Health Engineering;
Director, Hon, Institute of Medicinal Plant,
Chinese Academy of Medical Sciences

July 30, 1998

Preface

If somebody asks me what is the most precious thing in the world, I at once answer, health.

A friend of mine is a rich businessman. One day, when we were talking, I said, "You are so lucky. You have a lot of money. You can do anything you like." But he said, " I would rather exchange all of my money for my health." Indeed, without good health to enjoy it, what good are all the riches of the world. The key question remains how can we maintain our health?

In my opinion, good health starts our mind. The body follows the mind like a shadow, always turning where it turns, stopping when it stops. The mind makes all the decisions that either build or destroy health. If you choose to watch TV instead of taking a walk, your body is affected. If you take a high-pressure job, your body will suffer from the effects of stress. So, we earn our health. We reap what we sow.

Nowadays, prevention of diseases and maintaining good health by means of functional food and dietary supplements have become a trend and been taken seriously by professors and researchers in the medical field.

Chinese functional food is developed on the basis of the food therapy of Chinese medicine. It has attracted a great deal of international attention because of China's long medical history, unique food therapy theory, extensive Chinese materia medica resources and interest in oriental culture.

Some foods can be used to prevent and even treat diseases like medicine. Why? Let's take garlic (*Allium sativum L.*), a common food, as an example. In addition to such nutrients as protein, carbohydrates, vitamins, calcium, phosphorus, etc., garlic contains a volatile ingredient named allicin which can kill bacteria.

To demonstrate its bacteriocidal effect, mash the garlic and filter it, take some garlic juice and drop it into culture dishes containing Staphylococcal dysentery, Escherichia coli, Hemophilus pertussis, Aflatoxin. Several days later, it can be seen that the bacteria on which the garlic juice had been dropped has disappeared, while some colonies appear on the areas with no garlic juice. Even aflatoxin, which can produce a very strong substance, a cancer agent, was eliminated by garlic juice. From this test we can see that garlic is not only a food rich in nutrients but also a medicine which will kill bacteria.

Let's take radish, a common vegetable, as another example. Not only can it be cooked into very delicious dishes, but can also be used as medicine. For treating some symptoms like indigestion due to over-eating, abdominal distention and so on, radish proves to be effective, because there is a kind of oil with pungent and hot taste named mustard seed oil in white radish, which can promote the movement of stomach and small intestine, hence promote digestion, improve appetite and regulate *qi*. In addition, fried shredded radish with beef has the functions of reinforcing the spleen and stomach, strengthening tendon and bone, promoting the circulation of blood and eliminating sputum, etc.

A mixture of sliced radish and garlic paste invigorates the stomach, relieves dyspepsia, and eliminates phlegm. So it can be used to treat indigestion and high blood pressure.

"Xin Li Mei," a kind of sweet radish with green peel and red core, is treasured as ideal vegetable during such dry seasons as winter and early spring. So there is an old saying in China, "If you eat more radish in winter and more ginger in summer, you needn't see the doctor."

In addition, foods rich in fiber can prevent and treat ailments in the stomach and intestines, and especially help to prevent cancer of the colon and rectum.

Let's take Indian corn as another example. Indian corn is rich in nutrients. The fat contained in Indian corn is 4-5 times that of rice and flour, and the fat in corn is rich in unsaturated fatty acid, especially for linoleic acid which is 6 times higher than pig fat and 2 percent higher than peanut oil. So its consumption can reduce serum cholesterol and prevent high blood pressure.

Recent research has proved that Indian corn has an anti-cancer function. The fiber in Indian corn can promote the movement of stomach and small intestine. It can remove carcinogenic material and help to prevent cancer of the intestine.

Indian corn also contains glutathione. This can catch or hold the substances that cause cancer just like handcuffs and then excrete them out through the digestive tract.

Many clinical cases have proven that many food of the Chinese materia medica have an anti-cancer function, for instance: lentinus (*Lentinus Edodes*), meadow mushroom (*Agaricus Campestris*), water chestnut (*Pulpa Trapae*), tea (*Camellia sinensis*), bean sprout (*Semen Sojae Germinatum*), Job's Tears (*Coix lacryma-jobi var. ma-yuen*), soybean (*Glycine max*), Chinese jujube (*Ziziphus jujuba*), fruit of Chinese wolfberry (*Lycium barbarum*), poria, (*Poria*), Chinese caterpillar fungus (*Cordyceps*), fruit of seabuckthorn (*Fructus Hippophae*), lingchih (*Ganoderma*), umbellate pore fungus (*Ployporus*), rhizome of wild buckwheat (*Radix Fagopyri Cymosi*), curcuma (*Curcuma longa*), arnebia root (*Lithospermum erythrorhizon*), common fig (*Fructus Fici*), etc.

Cow's milk or ewe's milk is not only rich in various kinds of vitamins, but also contains certain cancer-preventing substances; fresh vegetables such as radish, cabbage, pumpkin, pea, lettuce, carrots, spinach, and tomato, are all rich in vitamin A and have a certain cancer-preventing effect.

Several components of plant foods inhibit a variety of tumors in various tissues. Take soybeans for example, the consumption of soy products has been associated with low rates of hormone dependent and hormone-independent cancers. Asians, who consume 20-50 times more soy per capita than Americans, have lower incidence and lower death rates from breast and prostate cancer.

In addition, by eating more fruit and vegetables which are green, red and yellow, one can replenish a lot of carotene and vitamin C, therefore, curing some diseases caused by lack of vitamins. This has become common knowledge for modern people.

Some people overwork, eat rich overcooked foods, abuse alcohol and have too little sleep. They don't realize that their lifestyle affects their health. Medicine is not the solution to a disease-causing lifestyle. Some people consider enough meat and occasional vegetable for lunch to be what they need to stay healthy. It isn't that simple.

Recent research on food components that may reduce the risk of some cancers — and consumer and health professionals' attitudes towards such a concept – indicates physicians and dietitians may need to "catch up" with scientific advances and the strong consumer interest in "functional foods."

This book includes seven chapters: History of Chinese Functional Food; Current Status of Chinese Functional Food; Characteristics and Theory of Chinese Functional Food; Classification of Chinese Functional Food; Food-and-Medicines Approved in China; and Application of Chinese Functional Food.

"Health for all by the year 2000" is the global strategic goal put forward by WHO. The promotion of functional food is one of the most effective vehicles of realizing this goal.

Dang Yi
July 1998

Chapter 1

History of Chinese Functional Food

1.1 Pre-Qin Period (Before 207 B.C.)

Chinese functional food has a long history in China. In searching for food, man discovered medicinal substances. China has an ancient saying that medicine and food have the same origin. In the beginning, primitive people ate wild fruit and seeds and dug up the roots of plants to appease their hunger. When they gathered wild fruits, they could not tell what was food and what was medicine. To satisfy their hunger, they often ate poisonous plants which would lead to vomiting, loose bowels and giddiness or even death and others that could help them get well when they were sick. Out of these experiences, they gradually learnt to identify plants that would cause vomiting or diarrhea, those that were poisonous, those that were harmful and those that were beneficial to the body. So gradually people came to know some plant medicines.

The discovery of fire must be mentioned when dealing with the origin of health care as primitive man's use of fire played an important role in protecting health. The invention of fire brought light and warmth, and people learnt to cook their food. Animal bones and stones found among the ashes indicate that primitive people often roasted animal meat in their caves. Fire changed primitive man's eating habits. Cooked food was much easier to digest and better for mental and physical development. The body was able to absorb more nutrition from the food, thus decreasing the incidence of some diseases and strengthening man's constitution.

Primitive people got to know about animal medicine from their hunting activities. They learnt that gall bladder could loosen the bowels and that liver was good for the eyes. Even today people of Oroqen ethnic group still have the habit of taking out the gall bladders from the animals they have just shot and eating them raw. They believe that this will give them very clear eyesight.

Primitive people eventually discovered the therapeutic effects of animal fat, blood, bone marrow and offal in treating diseases. As was recorded in *The Classics of Mountains and Seas*, "There is a kind of fish called Heluo which can be used to treat carbuncles." *The Classics of Mountains and Seas* is a famous geographical work of ancient China. Based on oral legends, it was probably written in the fifth century B.C. Supplements were written by later generations; it was not the work of one person or completed within a short period. It consists mainly of folklore concerning geographical knowledge and also includes some pharmaceutical knowledge.

Archaeologists have found the husks of millet, rice, and other cereals, and the seeds of cabbage and mustard in the jars and other relics in caves used by primitive people in Shaanxi and Zhejiang provinces, proving that China has a very long history of growing and eating cereals and vegetables.

The constant enlargement of the sources of food and the continuous increase in varieties of food helped promote better health in primitive society.

During the pre-Qin period, food therapy began to take shape. Many history books recorded that the people in the Yin Dynasty drank wine. During that time, the wine offered in the sacrifices to the Gods was "Chang," a fragrant herbal wine made by more than 100 kinds of herbal grass. In the book *Shuo Wen Dictionary,* a classic Chinese dictionary, the word "醫" (i.e., treatment) was explained by "wine," showing wine was used to cure diseases. The ancient character "醫" for doctor is made up of three component parts. At the top of the left corner is the radical for a quiver of arrows; at the right-hand corner a hand grasping a weapon and below the symbol for sorcerer or priest. Later however the third part of the symbol was changed to wine, signifying that the practice of medicine was no longer confined to the priests but had been taken up by doctors who administered elixirs or wines to their patients (see Fig. 1).

Fig. 1   Chinese Character Meaning Medicine/Doctor
Divided into Its Component Parts

China has a long history of brewing wine, the origin of which can be traced back to primitive society. With the development of primitive agriculture, grain in storage would sometimes sprout and go moldy, thus causing saccharification and fermentation resulting in alcohol and "natural wine" formation. People gradually found that drinking this "natural wine" made the whole body feel warm and caused mental excitation.

Yin people knew how to use certain food to cure illnesses. From the inscriptions on oracle bones and turtle shells found in the Yin ruins, we can see that fish had been used to cure stomach diseases. Legend has it that during Shang Dynasty (c. 17th century-11th century B.C.) a certain emperor Tang had a minister named Yi Yin. This minister was an excellent cook, and also understood the properties of foods. Very often he would himself prepare soups and decoctions to cure the sick. He had some medical knowledge, and when preparing meals, he discovered the effect of some condiments, such as ginger, cinnamon, and jujube. By combining his experience in using herbs with the methods used in cooking, he boiled the herbs in water to produce a liquid. Therefore, the appearance of the decoction method is directly related to the improvement of food preparation techniques. He wrote *The Soup and Decoctions,* the earliest book on food therapy, thus becoming the father of food therapy. Later, people memorialized him by coining the term "Yi Yin Soup and Decoctions."

As early as the Western Zhou Dynasty (c. 11th century-771 B.C.), there already were food doctors. According to the book of *The Rites of the Zhou Dynasty*, there were four kinds of professional physicians at that time in China, namely food doctor, physician (or doctors of internal medicine), surgeon and veterinary doctor. The food doctor's responsibilities were to prepare meals for the emperor and to help maintain the health of the members of the imperial court. Physicians were in charge of the treatment of internal diseases while the surgeon took care of traumas such as sores and fractures. And the veterinary doctor treated the diseases of the livestock. The food doctors were given the leading position, for they were considered as the most important. These food doctors at that time were the earliest nutritionists in the world.

The Inner Canon of the Yellow Emperor sums up the theory of food therapy, by stating that a proper diet is most important for maintaining health of the body and that an uncontrolled diet is an important cause of diseases. In the book The Inner Canon of the Yellow Emperor, herbal wine is described as being able to cure chronic and serious illnesses, and encouraged patients to cooperate during rehabilitation by eating as much cereal, meat, fruit and vegetable as possible. That is, restoring the vital energy by means of eating and drinking. The Basic Questions Section of The Inner Canon of the Yellow Emperor points out, "Grains are for growth, fruits for assistance, meats for nourishment and vegetables for supplements. If all of these are served together at one meal, they will fortify the essence of life and benefit qi." It went on to explain that foods could be used as medicines.

1.2   Han Dynasty (206 B.C.-220 A.D.)

Prescriptions for Fifty-Two Kinds of Diseases unearthed from the No. 3 tomb of the Han Dynasty at Mawangdui, Changsha, Hunan Province in 1973 — the earliest extant medical works, recording about the medicated porridge for treatment. Ther are the oldest records and books in medicine and pharmacy.

It was recorded in Huai Nan Zi of Western Han Dynasty (206 B.C.-24 A.D.), a classic book about Chinese culture and history, that the ancient emperor Shen Nong was the father of agriculture. "After tasting all kinds of plants and spring water, Shen Nong told people which were good for them. There were times when he tasted wild plants and came across 70 varieties of poison in one day." Of course, Shen Nong is not a person but a name for primitive people. Primitive people got to know about animal medicine from their hunting activities. They learnt that gall bladder could loosen the bowels and that liver was good for the eyes.

Shen Nong's Classic of Herbalism is the earliest book about Chinese materia medica in China. It was completed in the early part of the first century A.D. (the last years of the Western Han Dynasty). It classified 365 Chinese materia medica into three grades: superior, intermediate and low. The superior-grade medicinal items are mostly of the nourishing and strengthening type, non-toxic and suitable for long-term administration, such as radix ginseng, fructus jujubae and fructus lycii. The intermediate-grade includes both toxic and non-toxic ones, such as radix astragali, bulbus lilii, which, when used properly, have a curative effect and can strengthen a weak body. The low-grade medicinal items are powerful, toxic ones which can be used to treat severe cases. At least half of the Chinese materia medica in this book can be used as medicine or food, such as Chinese jujube, lotus root, grape, Chinese yam, honey, orange, longan, sesame, etc. With the development of traditional Chinese medicine (TCM), many papers and books about food have been published. Up to now, it is still difficult to divide foods from herbs.

In the Eastern Han Dynasty (25-220), Zhang Zhongjing (150-219), also named Zhang Ji, a famous doctor and the author of *Treatises on Febrile and Miscellaneous Diseases* and *Synopsis of Prescriptions of the Golden Chamber*, was able to cure chronic diseases through the use of Chinese materia medica combined with food. He used red bean and angelica powder to cure *huhuo* illness (狐惑), an ancient term for a disease resembling Behcet's syndrome, and he cured consumptive illnesses and "coldness" using Chinese yam. He cured poor appetite using lily egg soup and used thin porridge to strengthen the effect of the herbal medicine used. He stated that individual therapeutics implied not only a special consultation for each patient carried out according to one's own opinion and the treatment and prescriptions would be constantly modified in accordance with any pathological changes, if necessary, several times in the course of a day. Such prescriptions are still commonly used today in a decoction.

In his book, Zhang Zhongjing wrote that of the more than 200 members in his family, two-thirds died in less than 10 years, among which 70 percent died from febrile diseases. Faced with the widespread epidemics and the successive deaths of his relatives, Zhang felt the heavy responsibility of a doctor, and he made up his mind to work on the theory and methods of treating exogenous febrile diseases. He "diligently studied ancient teachings and made use of formulas of different schools." And finally wrote his books *Treatises on Febrile and Miscellaneous Diseases* and *Synopsis of Prescriptions of the Golden Chamber.*

1.3 Tang Dynasty (618-907)

Sun Simiao, a famous doctor in the Tang Dynasty, wrote a book named *Essentially Treasured Prescriptions* with a chapter entitled "Food Therapy" which mentioned the functions of 154 kinds of food including fruit, vegetable, grain and bird, beast, worm and fish. A literal translation of the title of the book *Essentially Treasured Prescriptions* (also called *Essentially Treasured Prescriptions for Emergencies*) would be *Prescriptions Worthy a Thousand Pieces of Gold.* Sun Simiao believed that human lives were more precious than money, thus the title of his book.

One of Sun Simiao's contributions was that he acquired much experience in food therapy and health preservation. Both in theory and practice, Sun Simiao earnestly followed the academic ideas he advocated. In this book, Sun Simiao pointed out: "Doctors should first understand the pathogenesis of the disease, and then treat it with food. Drugs should only be used if food therapy fails." He said that animal liver would cure night blindness. That vitamin A can cure night blindness was known only in modern times. For goiter patients, Sun prescribed lamb cheeks or deer cheeks. For edema patients, Sun prescribed grain husks which contained a lot of vitamin B. His research in this field made possible the prevention of illness due to malnutrition. People inscribed his prescriptions on stone tablets which spread them far and wide.

In the Tang Dynasty, the first publication of food therapy book, *Nourishing Prescriptions*, was written by Meng Shen (621-714), Sun Simiao's student. Meng Shen's students rewrote and made additions to the book, and retitled it *Herbalism of Food Therapy*. Meng Shen was a medical scientist whose long life itself is an indication of his achievements in the science of health preservation and food therapy. He studied and showed special interest in medical prescriptions even when he was a boy. Until his death at 93, he taught medicine and worked especially hard at researching on food therapy.

In the seventh century (657), the court of the Tang Dynasty organized Su Jing and 20 other people to compile and publish *Newly Revised Herbalism* for use throughout the country. It is the earliest state-issued pharmacopoeia. The classifications in *Newly Revised Herbalism* are based on the natural sources of the items and consisted of 11 categories: stones, plants, substances from the human body, animals, fowls, insects, fish, fruit, cereals, vegetables, and items which were listed but not used. The book also gives detailed accounts of the properties, origins, functions, and indications of the items.

1.4 Song Dynasty (960-1279)

During the Song Dynasty, it was very popular to prevent and treat diseases with functional food. For instance, *Prescriptions of the Taiping Period* compiled by imperial court, recorded 28 kinds of diseases that can be treated by food prescriptions. *Imperial Medical Encyclopedia*, another book published in the Song Dynasty, has a chapter on food therapy including 30 sections. These two books illustrate a total of 330 recipes for food therapy with medicated porridge, such as fresh ginger porridge for the treatment of cold, seed of spine date porridge for insomnia, Welsh onion stalk porridge for dysentery, India pokeberry porridge for edema, and desert-living cistanche and sheep kidney porridge for general debility, etc. *Shan Jia Qing Gong*, written by Lin Hong, recorded 102 kinds of vegetable dishes for the treatment of illness and maintaining health. *Yang Lao Feng Qin Shu*, written by Chen Zhi, contained 162 food prescriptions for old people.

1.5 Yuan Dynasty (1271-1368)

During the Yuan Dynasty, Wu Rui wrote *the Materia Medica for Daily Use*. Soon after its publication, the imperial court's food doctor Hu Sihui wrote the book *Orthodox Essentials of Dietetics*. He was a Chinese Mongolian and his outstanding work is representative of the period. These two books each have their own special qualities and are based on different principles and approaches to the concept of food therapy. However, they shared the common concept of "food fortifying" in healthy persons. This formed the basis for Chinese clinical medicine's nutritional work. In addition, *Orthodox Essentials of Dietetics* advanced the development of the study of the medicinal aspects of regular foodstuffs. It is mainly a study of the use of nutrition to maintain health,

Hu Sihui believing that it was better to pay attention to nutrition before the onset of a disease than to rely on medicine to cure disease after its onset. The main part of his book introduces foods which have replenishing effects and the use of herbs in preparing ordinary foods. It also deals with the properties and functions of some everyday food, and gives examples of some nutritious food and cooking methods. The book also includes descriptions of food frequently eaten by the people of the Mongolian, Han, Hui, and Tibetan ethnic groups in China and discusses their value in nutriology. The book also includes more than 20 drawings and a large number of food recipes of traditional functional food.

1.6　Ming Dynasty (1368-1644)

Li Shizhen (1518-93), also named Dongbi, a great pharmacologist and a famous doctor in the Ming Dynasty, had studied several thousand species of animals and plants both north and south of the Yangtze River. After 27 years of hard work, he collected more than 500 kinds of herbs for food therapy in his book named *The Great Herbalism (Compendium of Materia Medica)*. Li's book is the most outstanding and comprehensive work on Chinese materia medica. It was published in 1590 in 52 volumes and listed 1,892 medicinal substances. There were more than 1,000 illustrations and over 10,000 prescriptions with detailed descriptions. These included the appearance, properties, collection methods, preparation and use of each substance. It is arranged into 16 classes: water, fire, earth, metals, minerals, herbs, cereals, vegetables, fruits, trees, garments and utensils, insects, fishes, molluscs, birds, beasts and men. His work is a classic and is still studied today by traditional practitioners.

1.7 Qing Dynasty (1644-1911)

In Qing Dynasty, functional food in Chinese medicine developed very quickly. Many books about food therapy were published, including the 12-volume *Complete Herbalism of Food* written by Shen Lilong; *Menu of Sui Yuan* by Yuan Zicai; *Yin Shi Shi Er He Lun* by Zhang Ying; *Tiao Ji Yin Shi Bian* by Zhang Xingyun; *Shi Wu Mi Shu* by Chen Xiuyuan; *Sui Xi Ju Yin Shi Pu* by Wang Shixiong; *Fei Shi Shi Yang* by Fei Boxiong and *A Supplement to the Great Herbalism* by Zhao Xuemin.

It should be noted that China is a multi-minority country with 56 ethnic groups. Besides the Han ethnic group, many other ethnic groups, including the Tibetan, Mongolian, Hui, Miao, Korean, Oroqen, and Dai, all have their own medicine, food therapy and functional food.

In general, over Chinese history, many books on food therapy and functional food have been written. Today, unfortunately, only 50 or so books remain (see Table 1).

Chinese medical doctors in modern times advocate the development of functional food. Along with China's reform and opening to the outside world, the general living standard of the public had risen progressively from subsistence to modestly well-to-do. The increasingly demanding from the dressing market serves as the main force behind the development of functional food. Functional food factories amounted to less than 100 in 1980, and rapidly increased to more than 3,000 in 1992. They produce over 3,000 varieties of functional foods, with an annual output value of 20 billion yuan Rmb, about 10 percent of the food industry. The total sales of functional food in that year were over 450 million yuan in Beijing alone.

In early years of the 1990s, function food production soared. As the functional food production became industrialized and modernized and on a corporation scale of operation, a large number of brands and highly

Table 1	A Brief Chronology on Chinese Functional Food		
Dynasty	**Achievement**	**Published**	**Author**
Pre-history	1.People gradually discovered some medicinal herbs when collecting food. 2.The discovery of fire.		
Shang Dynasty (c.17th century-c.11th century B.C.)	1. Invention of herbal wine. 2. Treatment stomach disease with fish. 3. Decoction began to be used to treat diseases in the early part of the Shang Dynasty (according to the preface of *A-B Classic of Acupuncture and Moxibustion:* "Yi Yin made decoctions").	The inscriptions on oracle bones and turtle shells Tang Ye Jing	Yi Yin
Western Zhou Dynasty (c. 11th century-771 B.C.)	Occupation of food doctor	*The Rites of the Zhou Dynasty*	Zhou Gong
Spring and Autumn and Warring States periods (770-21B.C.)	Established the basic theory of TCM	*The Inner Canon of the Yellow Emperor*	
Eastern Han Dynasty (25-220)	Cure of chronic diseases with Chinese materia medica combined with food.	*Treatises on Febrile and Miscellaneous Diseases* and *Synopsis of Prescriptions of the Golden Chamber*	Zhang Zhongjing,

Tang Dynasty (618-907)	The first chapter entitled "Food Therapy."	*Essentially Treasured Prescriptions for Emergencies*	Sun Simiao,
	The first book entitled *Food Therapy.*	*Herbalism of Food Therapy*	Meng Shen
Song Dynasty (960-1279)	Recorded 28 kinds of diseases treated by food prescriptions.	*Imperial Benevolent Prescriptions of the Taiping Period*	Wang Huaiyin, *et. al.*
	Has a chapter of "Food Therapy" including 30 sections.	*The Imperial Medical Encyclopedia*	Zhao Ji
	Recorded 102 kinds of vegetable dishes for treatment and maintaining health.	*Vegetable Meals of Hill Inhabitants*	Lin Hong
	Collected 162 food prescriptions for old people	*Health Care of Parents and Old People*	Chen Zhi
Yuan Dynasties (1206-1368)	These two books have their own benefits, and each concept of food therapy. They both add the concept of "food fortifying" in healthy persons.	*Materia Medica for Daily Use*	Wu Rui
		Orthodox Essentials of Dietetics	Hu Sihui
Ming Dynasty (1368-1644)	Including 16 classes: water, fire, earth, metals, minerals, herbs, grains, vegetables, fruits, trees, garments and utensils, insects, fishes, molluscs, birds, beasts and men.	*Compendium of Materia Medica (or The Great Herbalism)*	Li Shizhen

Qing Dynasty (1644-1911)	In Qing Dynasty, functional food in Chinese medicine developed very quickly. A lot of books about food therapy were published	*Compiled of Herbalism of Food*	Shen Lilong
		Recipes for Sui Yuan	Yuan Zicai
		Twelve Comments on Diet	Zhang Ying
		Food Therapy for Common Diseases	Zhang Xingyun
		Secret Book of Food	Chen Xiuyuan
		Cookbook for Food & Drinks in Daily Life	Wang Shixiong
		Fei's Health Preserving by Food	Fei Boxiong
		A Supplement to the Great Herbalism	Zhao Xuemin

competitive products have been developed. Moreover, a number of large and middle-sized new enterprises and corporations with an annual output value from 100 million to even 1 billion yuan have emerged for producing brand products that are recognized and acclaimed across the country.

In recent years, research work on functional food has gained increasing attention both at home and abroad. The outcome of these research efforts shows that functional food products have a protective effect on health, assist in recuperation from illness and enhance the immunity of the body. Production of healthy ingredients through maximization of secondary metabolite production in plants, stabilization of fish oils to produce products such as mayonnaise and margarine with

14

bioactive lipids; development of technologies to maximize positive physiological effects of foods and their components, maximization of mineral bioavailability through physicochemical interactions in food and process optimization, molecular modification of food components to maximize physiological effects; inhibition of the formation of toxic end products in processed and stored foods; stabilization of physiologically beneficial compounds in foods, etc.

Many research results of functional food by the experts and scholars show that heightened standards of strength and health result directly from the effects of taking functional food. Traditional Chinese medicine is considered one of the miracles in the history of science. It occupies an important place in the rich Chinese national heritage. It is a great treasure house indeed.

Chapter 2

Current Status of
Chinese Functional Food

Article 22 of the Law of Food Hygiene, enacted by the Standing Committee of the Chinese National People's Congress on October 30, 1995, stipulates that any food product or its specification claiming functions for health must be submitted to the Ministry of Public Health under the State Council for examination. The Ministry of Public Health will examine the hygienic standard as well as the production, marketing, and management of the food products. The Measures Concerning Administration of Functional Food have been enforced since June 1, 1996 to regulate the use, examination, production, marketing and sales, labeling, specification, advertising, and monitoring of functional food in China.

2.1   Concept and Definition of Functional Food

The concept and definition of functional food are very difficult to determine.   They are still to be settled after being debated for decades. The definitions of functional food are different from country to country. The term "functional food" was first used in Japan and is now widely used in the Europe and America[1-2]. The earliest definition by Japanese Public Health Ministry in 1962 is as follows:

"Functional food is the food which comprises a kind of functional factor relating to biological protection, biological rhythmic regulation, disease prevention and health restoration, has been processed, and has a significant effect on the regulation of body functions [3]."

Basically, functional food is: (1) made from raw materials or ingredients of daily food; (2) taken in the diet in the usual way; and (3) labeled to specify its function in biological regulation [3]. Functional food is commonly understood in Korea as "therapeutic food," as appreciated in IUFOST ' 96 Regional Symposium on Non-Nutritive Health Factors for Future Foods [4], which was sponsored by South Korea' s Food Science Technology Society. "Health food" and "pharm food"[5] are also common terms for functional food in the United States. The term "improvement food" is commonly used in Germany.

According to the World Food Research Institute, there are two categories of health food, i.e., natural health food and prescribed health food.

Natural health food comprises:

(1) The food for good health (narrow scope), which helps maintain and improve health;

(2) Natural food, which is free of food additives; and

(3) Nutritional supplement food, which is nutrition supplements and modifiers.

Prescribed functional food may be also used for therapeutic and corrective purposes. In China, it is called medicated food [6], medicated diet[7], therapeutic food, food for health care, food for maintaining health[8], diet for nutrition, food for nutrition and health care[9], etc. Old terms such as imperial diet[10], rare diet[11], food recipe for therapy, etc. are also widely used [12-14].

In spite of the great differences in nomenclature and classification of functional food in different countries, a consensus is to focus on the function for health care, the so-called the third function of food. These measures provide such a unified concept of Chinese functional food. As stipulated in Article 2 of Chapter 1 of the measures, functional food is the food with specific functions for health care. Functional food is suitable for use by specific groups of people to improve their body functions but it is not aimed at treating diseases [15].

In a word, a good definition for functional foods is this: they are foods which can be part of our everyday diet but which have properties that provide an additional benefit for health.

2.2 Requirements for Examination of Functional Food

To implement scientific examination measures and standardize functional foods, the Ministry of Public Health has established the Committee of Food Hygiene Examination and promulgated a series of rules and regulations, including Rules of Technology in Functional Food Examination, Evaluation and Examination Methods for Functional Food, Rules of Functional Food Labeling, and General Requirements of Functional Food Hygiene. Responsible governments in different municipalities, provinces and autonomous regions authorized some institutes to conduct testing of functional food. Without the formal approval by the Ministry of Public Health or an application submitted to the Health Administration under the State Council, any production, marketing, or sales under the name of functional food is illegal and will be prosecuted according to the Law of Food Hygiene. As yet, about 2,000 Chinese functional food items have been approved by the Ministry of Public Health and entitled to have a Logo of Functional Food on their packages (see Fig. 2).

2.3 Evaluation and Testing of Functional Food

Before the promulgation of the rules, it was difficult to have standard methods for functional food testing. Common Standards for Functional Food were published by the National Technology Supervision Bureau on February 28, 1997 and have been enforced since May 1, 1997.

18

Fig. 2   The Logo of Chinese Functional Food

保健食品

* The logo issued by the Ministry of Public Health is in sky blue color.

At present, the authorized institutes for testing functional food need to perform 24 tests on functional food products:

- Immune regulation
- Postponement of senility
- Memory improvement
- Promotion of growth and development
- Anti-fatigue
- Body weight reduction
- Oxygen deficit tolerance
- Radiation protection
- Anti-mutation
- Anti-tumor
- Blood lipid regulation
- Sex potency improvement
- Blood glucose regulation
- Gastro-intestinal function improvement
- Sleep improvement

- Improvement of nutritional anemia
- Protection of liver from chemical damages
- Lactation improvement
- Improvement for beauty
- Vision improvement
- Promotion of lead removal
- Removal of "intense heat" from the throat and moistening of the throat
- Blood pressure regulation
- Enhancement of bone calcification

The published standards avoid arbitrary descriptions of the functions of functional food. For examining any functional food which has not yet been classified by standards, functional food manufacturers could propose some testing and evaluation methods. The proposed methods will be verified by the experts assigned by the Ministry of Public Health before acceptance and listing of the methods in the standards [16].

Regarding the appearance and other sensory characteristics, the standards stipulate that functional food must have defined shape, color, smell, taste, and quality. Any annoying smell or taste is not allowed.

In addition, China National Technical Standardization Committee of Food Industry has proposed the standards. Take *The General Standard for the Labeling of Foods* for example. The general principles are as follows:

1. Prepackaged food shall not be described or presented on any label or in any labeling in a manner that is false, misleading or deceptive.

2. Prepackaged food shall not be described or presented on any label or in any labeling by words, pictorial or other devices which refer to or are suggestive either directly or indirectly, of any other product or any

characteristics of any other product with which such food might be confused.

3. Prepackaged food shall be described or presented on any label or in any labeling according to the requirements of the state laws and regulations, and related product standards.

4. Prepackaged food shall be described or presented on any label or in any labeling by words, pictorial or other devices, popularly, precisely and scientifically.

Let's take *Labeling of Foods for Special Nutrient* for another example. The general principles are:

In addition to compliance with *General Principles of the General Standard for the Labeling of Foods*, the labeling for special nutrients shall comply with the following principles:

1. The calorific value and the quantity of the nutrients contained with the date of minimum durability of a food shall be declared.

2. The following information should not be declared on any label:

1) Any claims as to the prevention or treatment of a disease,

2) Any claims as to "the recovery of one's youthful vigor," "prolongation of life," "change hoary hairs to black," "new teeth regrowing in the gums of fallen teeth," "anti-cancer or curing a cancer," and so on.

3) Any claims as to "a secret prescription of a food handed down in the family from generation to generation," "nourishing food," "food for improvement of health and beauty," "food of prescription used in imperial palace," and so on.

4) Any declaration of drug name either immediately before or after the name of a food, or the pictorial or name of a drug implying the effects of treatment, health care, or similar effects of such foods.

2.4 Extension of Functional Food to Chinese Medicine Prescriptions

Distinguishing between functional food and traditional Chinese medicine is not an easy task. It is difficult to tell which is functional food and not Chinese medicine, or vice versa. It has been long believed that food and medicine share a common origin in Chinese tradition. To resolve this problem, the Ministry of Public Health has formally recognized 69 items as both food and Chinese medicine[17]. These 69 items of dietary Chinese medicine are listed as follows (see Table 2).

Table 2   69 Food-and-Medicine Approved in China

Drug Latin Name	Chinese Name	English Name	Latin Name
Agkistrodon	蝮蛇，Fushe	Pallas Pit Viper	*Agkistrodon halys*
Arillus Longan	龙眼肉，Longyanrou	Longan Aril	*Dimocarpus longan*
Bulbus Allii Macrostemi	薤白，Xiebai	Longstamen Onion Bulb	*Allium macrostemon*
Bulbus Lilii	百合，Baihe	Lily Bulb	*Lilium lancifolium; L. brownii var. viridulum; L. pumilum*
Concha Ostreae	牡蛎，Muli	Oyster Shell	*Ostrea gigas; O. talienwhanensis; O. rivularis*
Cortex Cinnamomi	肉桂，Rougui	Cassia Bark	*Cinnamomum cassia*
Endothelium Corneum Gigeriae Galli	鸡内金，Jineijin	Chicken's Gizzard-skin	*Gallus gallus domesticus*

22

Exocarpium Citri Rubrum	橘红，Juhong	Red Tangerine Peel	*Citrus reticulata*
Flos Carthami	红花，Honghua	Safflower	*Carthamus tinctorius*
Flos Caryophylli	丁香，Dingxiang	Clove	*Eugenia caryophylata*
Flos Chrysanthemi	菊花，Juhua	Chrysanthemun Flower	*Chrysanthemum morifolim*
Folium Mori	桑叶，Sangye	Mulberry Leaf	*Morus alba*
Folium Nelumbinis	荷叶，Heye	Lotus Leaf	*Nelumbo nucifera*
Folium Perillae	紫苏叶，Zisuye	Perilla Leaf	*Perilla frutescens*
Fructus Amomi	砂仁，Sharen	Villous Amomum Fruit	*Amomum villosum;* *A. villosum var. Xanthioides;* *A. longiligulare*
Fructus Anisi Stellati	八角茴香，Bajiaohuixiang	Chinese Star Anise	*Illcium verum*
Fructus Aurantii	代代花，Daidaihua	Orange Fruit	*Citrus aurantium `Daidai'*
Fructus Canarii	青果，Qingguo	Chinese White Olive	*Canarium album*
Fructus Cannabis	火麻仁，Huomaren	Hemp Seed	*Cannabis sativa*
Fructus Chaenomelis	木瓜，Mugua	Common Flowering-qince Fruit	*Chaenomeles speciosa*
Fructus Citri	香缘，Xiangyuan	Citron Fruit	*Citrus medica;* *C. wilsonii*
Fructus Citri Sarcodactylis	佛手，Foshou	Finger Citron	*Citrus medica var. sarcodactylis*
Fructus Crataegi	山楂，Shanzha	Hawthorn Fruit	*Crataegus pinnatifida var. major;* *C. pinnatifida*

23

Fructus Foeniculi	小茴香，Xiaohuixiang	Fennel	*Foeniculum vulgare*
Fructus Gardeniae	栀子，Zhizi	Cape Jasmine Fruit	*Gardenia jasminoides*
Fructus Hippophae	沙棘，Shaji	Seabuckthorn Fruit	*Hippophae rhamnoides*
Fructus Hordei Germinatus	麦芽，Maiya	Germinated Barley	*Hordeum vulgare*
Fructus Jujubae	大枣，Dazao	Chinese Date	*Ziziphus jujuba*
Fructus Lycii	枸杞子，Gouqizi	Barbary Wolfberry Fruit	*Lycium barbarum*
Fructus Momordicae	罗汉果，Luohanguo	Grosvenor Momordica Fruit	*Momordica grosvenori*
Fructus Mori	桑椹，Sangshen	Mulberry Fruit	*Morus alba*
Fructus Mume	乌梅，Wumei	Smoked Plum	*Prunus mume*
Fructus Piperis	胡椒，Hujiao	Pepper Fruit	*Piper nigrum*
Herba Cichorii	菊苣，Juju	Chicory Herb	*Cichorium glandulosum; C. intybus*
Herba Moslae	香薷，Xiangru	Haichow Elsholtzia Herb	*Mosla chinensis*
Herba Menthae	薄荷，Bohe	Peppermint	*Mentha haplocalyx*
Herba Pogostemonis	广藿香，Guanghuoxiang	Cablin Patchouli Herb	*Pogostemon cablin*
Herba Portulacae	马齿苋，Machixian	Purslane Herb	*Portulaca oleracea*

Mel	蜂蜜，Fengmi	Honey	Apis cerana; A. mellifera
Pericappium Citri Reticulatae	陈皮，Chenpi	Dried Tangerine Peel	Citrus reticulata
Pericarpium Zanthoxyli	花椒，Huajiao	Pricklyash Peel	Zanthoxylum schinifolium; Z. bungeanum
Poria	茯苓，Fuling	Indian Bread	Poria cocos
Radix Angelicae Dahuricae	白芷，Baizhi	Dahurian Angelica Root	Angelica dahurica; A. var. formosana
Radix Glycyrrhizae	甘草，Gancao	Liquorice Root	Glycyrrhiza uralensis; G. inflata; G. glabra
Rhizoma Apiniae Officinarum	高良姜，Gaoliangjiang	Lesser Galangal Rhizome	Alpinia officinarum
Rhizoma Dioscoreae	山药，Shanyao	Common Yam Rhizome	Dioscorea opposita
Rhizoma Imperatae	白茅根，Baimaogen	Lalang Grass Rhizome	Imperata cylindrica var. major
Rhizoma Phragmitis	芦根，Lugen	Reed Rhizome	Phragmites communis
Rhizoma Zingiberis Recens	生姜，Shengjiang	Fresh Ginger	Zingiber officinale
Semen Armeniacae Amarum	杏仁，Xingren	Apricot Seed	Prunus armeniaca var. ansu ; P. sibirica; P. mandshurica; P. armeniaca

Semen Canavaliae	刀豆，Daodou	Jack Bean	*Canavalia gladiata*
Semen Cassiae	决明子，Juemingzi	Cassia Seed	*Cassia obtusifolia; C. tora*
Semen Coicis	薏苡仁，Yiyiren	Coix Seed	*Coix lacrymajobi var. Ma-yuen*
Semen Euryales	芡实，Qianshi	Gordon Euryale Seed	*Euryale ferox*
Semen Ginkgo	白果，Baiguo	Ginkgo Seed	*Ginkgo biloba*
Semen Lablab Album	白扁豆，Baibiandou	White Hyacinth Bean	*Dolichos lablab*
Semen Myristicae	肉豆蔻，Roudoukou	Nutmeg	*Myristica fragrans*
Semen Nelumbinis	莲子，Lianzi	Lotus Seed	*Nelumbo nucifera*
Semen Persicae	桃仁，Taoren	Peach Seed	*Prunus persica; P. davidiana*
Semen Phaseoli	赤小豆，Chixiaodou	Rice Bean	*Phaseolus calcaratus; P. angularis*
Semen Pruni	郁李仁，Yuliren	Chinese Dwarf Cherry Seed	*Prunus humilis; Prunus japonica; P. pedunculata*
Semen Raphani	莱菔子，Laifuzi	Radish Seed	*Raphanus sativus*
Semen Sesami Nigrum	黑芝麻，Heizhima	Black Sesame	*Sesamum indicum*
Semen Brassicae Junceae	黄芥子，Huangjiezi	Yellow Mustard Seed	*Brassica juncea*
Semen Sojae Preparatum	淡豆豉，Dandouchi	Fermented Soybean	*Glycine max;*

Semen Torreyae	榧子，Feizi	Grand Torreya Seed	*Torreya grandis*
Semen Ziziphi Spinosae	酸枣仁，Suanzaoren	Spine Date Seed	*Ziziphus jujuba var. spinosa*
Thallus Laminariae	昆布，Kunbu	Kelp or Tangle	*Laminaria japonica*
Zaocys	乌梢蛇，Wushaoshe	Black Snake	*Zaocys dhumnades*

The number of items in the list will increase with further research and development of dietary Chinese medicine products, which must be safe, reliable, and with defined functions for health care.

The items which are not listed as dietary Chinese medicine require safety and toxicology evaluation, as stipulated in the Evaluation Methods and Testing Measures of Food Safety and Toxicology, before application for inclusion in the functional food listing.

2.5 Steady Development of Functional Food Products

As seen from the 2,000 kinds of food which had passed the functional food evaluation, current research and development of Chinese functional food has performed very well in formulation design, development of product categories, functions for health care, practical use, etc.

Formulation Design

Most of the approved functional food items were developed by using modern technology in accordance with modern nutritional science and nutritional knowledge of traditional Chinese medicine. Novel formulation and processes were found in the production of many functional food items. For example, the Tiao Zhi Ling (a golden remedy for regulating fat) comprises the fermentation liquid of hypha of Lingchih (*Ganoderma sp.*), honey, and fruits of Chinese wolfberry (*Lycium barbarum*).

Product Categories

The Chinese market for functional food has great potential. There are a variety of functional food products on the market in China. Effective functional food has been specially developed and produced for use by specific groups of people (e.g., specific races) under specific environment (e.g., geographical regions, climate, body conditions, etc.). The popular categories of functional food take the forms of health-care wine, health-care tea, health-care drinks, health-care vinegar, health-care cake, health-care powder, health-care rice, health-care flour, nutritional liquid, health-care chewing gum. In addition to local functional food products, foreign products such as shark's cartilage, melatonin, fish oil, spirulina have also entered China's functional food market.

Health-Care Functions

The vague terms such as "suitable for both the old and young," which is commonly used in the past, are not allowable. More definite terms such as "postponement of senility" and "immune regulation" are used instead.

According to our preliminary statistics, the most common health-care function categories are as follows:

• *Immune regulation*

西洋参 American ginseng (*Panax quinquefolius*)

人参 Ginseng (*Panax ginseng*)

刺五加 Acanthopanax (*Acanthopanax senticosus*)

枸杞子 Barbary wolfberry fruit (*Lycium barbarum*)

黄芪 Astragalus (*Astragalus membranaceus; A. Membranaceus var. Mongholicus*)

冬虫夏草 Chinese caterpillar fungus (*Cordyceps sinensis*)

银杏叶 Gingko leaf (*Ginkgo biloba*)

核桃仁 Walnut (*Juglans regia*)

大枣 Chinese date (*Ziziphus jujuba*)

蜂王浆 Royal jelly

当归 Chinese Angelica (*Angelica sinensis*)

灵芝 Glossy Ganoderma (*Ganoderma applanatum*)

* *Postponement of senility*

刺梨 Roxburgh rose (*Rosa roxburghii*)

绿茶 Green tea (*Camellia sinensis*)

何首乌 Fleeceflower root (*Polygonum multiflorum*)

黑芝麻 Black sesame (*Sesamum indicum*)

蜂蜜 Honey

桑椹 Mulberry fruit (*Morus alba*)

枸杞子 Barbary wolfberry fruit (*Lycium barbarum*)

* *Blood lipid regulation*

山楂 Hawthorn fruit (*Crataegus pinnatifida*)

大豆 Soybean (*Glycine max*)

桃仁 Peach seed (*Prunus persica*)

菊花 Chrysanthemum flower (*Chrysanthemum morifolium*)

高醋 super vinegar

酸枣仁 Spine date seed (*Ziziphus jujuba var. spinosa*)

鱼油 fish oil

玉米油 Corn oil (*Zea mays*)

亚麻籽油提取物 Extract of flax seed (*Linum usitatissimum*)

红花籽 Safflower seed (*Carthamus tinctorius*)

* *Blood and urine glucose reduction*

绞股蓝 Fiveleaf gynosttemma (*Gynostemma pentaphyllum*)

山楂 Hawthorn fruit (*Crataegus pinnatifida*)

山药 Chinese yam (*Dioscorea opposita*)

荞麦 Buckweat poria (*Fagopyrum esculentum*)

茯苓 Cocos poria (*Poria cocos*)

南瓜提取物 Extract of pumpkin (*Cucurbita moschata*)

猪胰提取物 Extract of pig pancreas

螺旋藻粉 Powder of spirulina (*Spirulina princeps*)

Other common function categories include anti-cancer, anti-fatigue, body weight reduction, sexual function improvement.

Practical Application

It is appreciated that legislation in China did not narrow the scope of functional food application. The approved functional food products include those suitable for the aged, children, men, and women in pregnancy and confinement after childbirth.

2.6 Trend and Prospects of Functional Food Development

With the rapid development of production technology and expected achievements in the near future, the quality of functional food products will be significantly improved. Consumers demand quality functional food for better nutrition, improvement of body functions, higher resistance to diseases. It is commonly believed that the 21st century will be the golden age for rapid development of functional food.

The market for functional food is huge and grows at a rapid rate. It was predicted that the gross sales of functional food will be 20 billion yuan in China market and US$22-24 billion in international market by the end of 20th century. Up until the 21st century, gross sales will increase at a rate of 15-20 percent per year. It's an exciting new field, and we can expect to see many new products!

Concluding Remarks

Long history and rich experience of traditional Chinese medicine in food therapy provides us with a number of traditional functional foods, e.g., *Herba Houttuyniae Houttuynia cordata Thunb.*, and Vaccinium bracteatum (*Vaccinium fragile Franch*). With the development of advanced technology, a new generation of Chinese functional food is emerging. In addition to human and animal testing for the effects of functional food on the body regulation, the structure and quantity of active ingredients of some functional food are also determined. The new generation of functional food will be of a higher quality and enjoy popularity in international markets.

References

1. Verschuren, Paulus M.1996, "Functional Food Science in Europe," Proceedings of IUFOSI '96 Regional Symposium on Non-Nutritive Health Factors for Future Foods, Seoul, Korea, pp. 25-26.

2. "Analysis and Perspective, Eastern and Western Scientists Share Perspectives on Functional Foods at International Conference," *World Food Regulation Review*, January 1996, pp. 17-19.

3. Jin Zonglian, 1995, *Evaluating Principles and Methods of Functional Food*, Beijing, Peking University Publishing House, pp. 1-2.

4. Cherl-Ho Lee, Health Concept in Traditional Korea Diet, Proceedings of IUFOSI '96 Regional Symposium on Non-Nutritive Health Factors for Future Foods, Seoul, Korea, pp. 47-56.

5. Etkin and John, 1996, "Medicated Food and Nutritious Agent: Transformation of Biological Therapy Model," a speech at International Symposium on Food Applied in Food and Medicine, London.

6. Wong Weijian, 1982, *A Collection of Choice Specimens of*

Medicated Diet Recipes, Beijing, the People's Medical Publishing House, p. 1.

7. Zhang Wengao, 1990, *Chinese Medicated Diet,* Shanghai, Publishing House of Shanghai College of Traditional Chinese Medicine, pp. 2-3.

8. Dang Yi, 1995, *Science of Nutrition Dietary Therapy of Traditional Chinese Medicine,* Beijing, Science Publishing House, p. 7.

9. Wong Weijian, 1992, *Nutriology of Traditional Chinese Medicine Diet,* Shanghai, Shanghai Science Publishing House, pp. 20-21.

10. Dang Yi, 1996, Medicated Diet Textual Research on the Term "Medicated Food," *Collection of Research Documents of TCM,* Beijing, TCM Classic Publishing House, pp. 168-171.

11. Hu Sihui, the Yuan Dynasty, *Principles of Correct Diet* (reprinted in 1987 by the People's Medical Publishing House, Beijing).

12. Chen Zhi, the Song Dynasty, *A New Book for Longevity and Health of the Aged* (reprinted in 1986 by China Bookstore, Beijing).

13. Sun Simiao, the Tang Dynasty, *Prescriptions Worth a Thousand Pieces of Gold for Emergencies* (reprinted in 1955 by the People's Medical Publishing House, Beijing).

14. Zhao Jie, the Song Dynasty, *Imperial Encyclopedia of Medicine* (reprinted in 1962 by the People's Medical Publishing House, Beijing).

15. The Ministry of Public Health of the People's Republic of China, 1996, *Measures of Functional Food Administration,* p. 16.

16. The Ministry of Public Health of the People's Republic of China, 1996, *The Functional Evaluating Process and Testing Measures of the Functional Food.*

17. Department of Hygiene Supervision of the Ministry of Public Health, 1997, *Collection of Administration Laws of the Functional Food,* Jilin Science and Technology Publishing House, p. 263.

Chapter 3
Characteristics and Theory of Chinese Functional Food

3.1 The Characteristics of Chinese Functional Food

3.1.1 Based on the Theory of TCM Which Includes:
- The concept of taking body as an organic whole (see 3.2.1).
- Treatment based on the differentiation of symptoms and signs (see 3.2.2).
- The theory of *yin* and *yang* (see 3.2.3).
- Theory of five elements (see 3.2.4).

3.1.2 Both Food and Chinese Materia Medica Come from Nature, Share the Same Theory and Can Be Used Together

Most of food and Chinese materia medica are taken from natural substances, animals, plants, etc., and they can be used together. Modern Chinese functional food is developed on the basis of the food therapy of Chinese medicine. The relationship of traditional Chinese functional food and modern Chinese functional food see Fig. 3.

In the Spring-Autumn Period, Confucius said, "No food removes poison from other food better than Bai Shao." That means, Bai Shao is the best thing to remove poison from food. And he said, "I would rather not eat a meal without the Bai Shao sauce." According to this record, the Chinese scholars made a drink of Bai Shao.

Fig. 3 The Relationship of Traditional Chinese Functional Food and Modern Chinese Functional Food

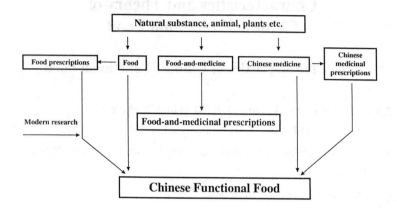

So from this example we also know that there are many ancient prescriptions which inspire modern research.

In addition, both food and Chinese materia medica have the same theory. For instance, the theory of Chinese materia medica is based on flavor, taste, lifting, lowering, floating and sinking. These are the properties of Chinese materia medica. Also the food has the same theory and properties as Chinese materia medica. Even they have the same theory pertaining the meridian.

3.1.3 Good in Taste, Convenient for Taking

Chinese people often say "Good medicine tastes bitter" because most of the decoctions of Chinese materia medica are bitter. Some people, especially children, do not like the bitter taste of Chinese materia medica and refuse to take it. Most of the Chinese materia medica used in medicated food are both edible and medicinal. They retain the properties of food, such as color, sweet-smell, and flavor, etc. Even if parts of them are Chinese materia medica, they can be made into tasty functional food by special cooking methods or being mixed with other food. So, functional food can be good in taste and convenient to take.

3.1.4 Suitable for Both Prevention and Treatment, Outstanding in Effect

Chinese functional food can be used to treat diseases, to improve health, and prevent diseases. This is one of the characteristics in which functional food is different from treatment by medicine. Although functional food is something mild, it has a notable effect on the prevention and cure of diseases, health building and health preserving.

Now, maybe some people say, "Well, I understand that functional food can be used to maintain health. We have to eat food for everyday nutrition. I also understand that functional foods can prevent diseases by their effective ingredients. But, I don't understand the principle of how Chinese functional food maintains health, prevents and even treats disease according to the theory of TCM."

How do you understand diseases? According to the theory of TCM, the general idea is that the *yin* and *yang* are out of balance. The principle of treatment in TCM is to regulate *yin* and *yang*, and to make the *yin* and *yang* balance.

What is the cause of the imbalance of *yin* and *yang*? Generally there are two aspects. One is the external cause and the other is the internal cause (see Fig. 4 and Fig. 5).

Let's take irregular diet in internal injury as an example. Food was literally called "water and grain" by the ancient Chinese. They are the source of the nutritive substances from which *qi* and blood are derived, and are indispensable for the maintenance of life processes. Irregular food intake is an important pathogenic factor. It should be eaten in proper

Fig. 4 The Causes of Exogeneous Diseases

The normal variations in the weather of the four seasons

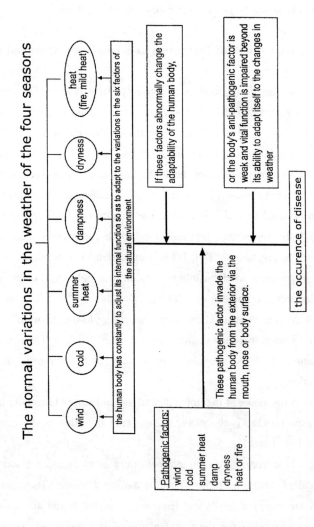

wind | cold | summer heat | dampness | dryness | heat (fire, mild heat)

the human body has constantly to adjust its internal function so as to adapt to the variations in the six factors of the natural environment

If these factors abnormally change the adaptability of the human body,

or the body's anti-pathogenic factor is weak and vital function is impaired beyond its ability to adapt itself to the changes in weather

Pathogenic factors:
wind
cold
summer heat
damp
dryness
heat or fire

These pathogenic factor invade the human body from the exterior via the mouth, nose or body surface.

the occurence of disease

To treat this kind of disease, we can use the way of removing the external pathogenic factors

Fig.5 The Causes Of Internal Diseases

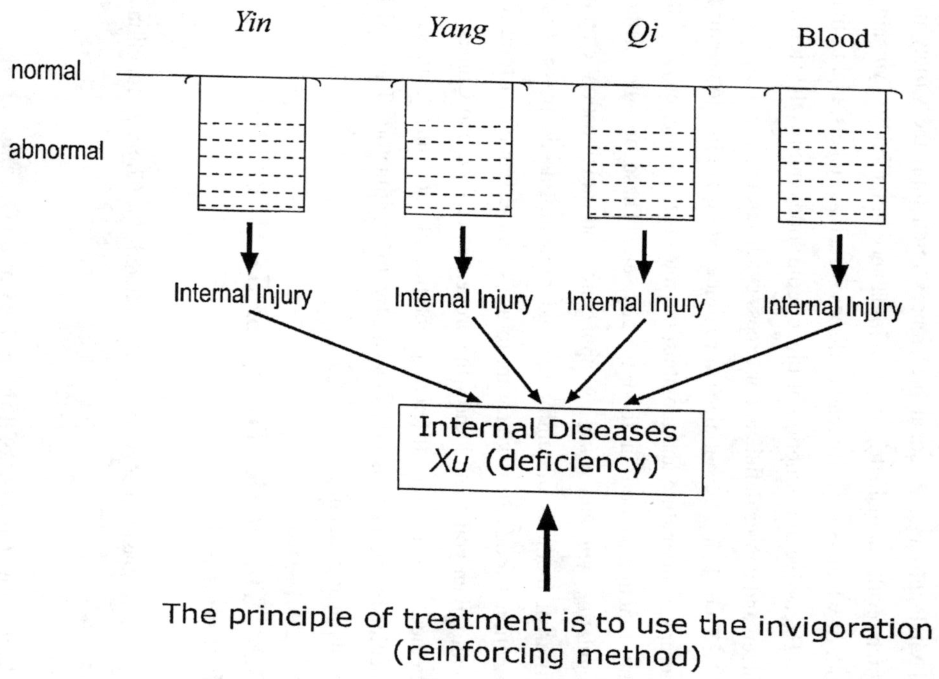

The principle of treatment is to use the invigoration (reinforcing method)

amounts at regular intervals: both insufficient food intake and over-eating can cause disease. Inadequate food intake leads to malnutrition.

A variety of foods should be taken to ensure that the body receives all vital nutrients. Personal preferences often limit the variety of diets which results in malnutrition or an imbalance in the body's *yin* and *yang*, both of which eventually lead to diseases such as rickets, night blindness, etc. Excessive consumption of raw or cold foods injures the stomach and spleen and causes deficiency or excess syndromes.

To make up for deficiency or reduce excess we like to use medicinal therapy, acupuncture and moxibustion, massage, *qigong*, physical therapy and functional food in food therapy, etc. These are the methods of regulating *yin* and *yang*. Acupuncture and moxibustion employ the different methods of reinforcing and reducing, as do massage and the functional food. So if you want to use Chinese functional food for your health, then you should know the properties of food and Chinese materia medica. We use the different properties of food and Chinese materia medica to regulate disorders caused by different factors. The next section explains it in detail.

3.2 The Basic Theory of TCM Related to Chinese Functional Food

The basic theory of TCM related to Chinese functional food includes:

3.2.1 The Concept of Taking Body as an Organic Whole

TCM attaches great importance to the unity of the human body itself and its relationship with nature, and holds that the human body itself is an organic whole and has very close and inseparable relations with the

38

external natural surroundings.

The human body is made up of *zang fu*, tissues and other organs. Each of them has their own special physiological functions. All these different physiological functions are components of the entire life process of the body. Therefore, the components of the human body are inseparable from each other in structure. They are related, supplementary and conditional to each other in physiology. They also influence each other in pathology. These mutual relations and influences are centered on the five viscera (the heart, the liver, the spleen, the lung and the kidney) and come into effect through the meridians and collaterals. For instance, the heart is interiorly and exteriorly related to the small intestine. It controls blood circulation, and has its "specific opening" in the tongue proper. So if a patient suffers from a headache, a Western medical doctor may give him drugs to stop the pain. But TCM physicians do not use Chinese materia medica for it, but find the cause and devise a method of treatment. The treatment for a headache that results from stagnation of blood will be very different from the headache due to insufficiency of blood.

The physiological interactions can become quite complex but the main physiological functions of the *zang* organs can be summarized as follows.

Heart:
- Houses the mind
- Controls blood and vessels
- Opens to the tongue

Liver:
- Stores blood
- Maintains patency for the flow of *qi*

- Controls the tendons
- Opens to the eye

Spleen:
- Governs transformation (digestion and absorption) and transportation
- Controls the blood in the vessels
- Dominates the muscles
- Opens to the mouth

Lung:
- Dominates qi and respiration
- Regulates water passages
- Dominates skin and hair
- Opens into the nose

Kidney:
- Stores essence and dominates reproduction, growth and development
- Produces marrow, forms the brain, and dominates the bones and the manufacture of blood
- Dominates water metabolism (clear and turbid water)
- Receives the qi
- Opens to the ear

Man lives in nature. Nature is vital for living. Changes in nature may cause physiological and pathological responses of human body.

The occurrence, development and changes of many diseases are seasonal (see Table 3).

Table 3 An Example of the Occurrence, Development and Changes of Diseases in Different Seasons

spring	more epidemic febrile diseases
summer	more sun strokes
autumn	more cases with symptoms of dryness
winter	more cold-stroke syndromes

TCM physicians have observed that the severity of some disease may change at different periods in a day, e.g., early morning, late afternoon, daytime and night.

TCM believes that different geographical surroundings affect the physiology and pathology of the human body. The effects are even capable of extending or shortening human life.

3.2.2 Treatment Based on the Differentiation of Symptoms and Signs

Different people need different functional foods. People living in different places with different climates and having different body constitutions need different functional foods.

Before prescribing functional food, we should first make a diagnosis by an overall analysis of patient's physical state and health, the nature of his illness, the season when he became ill and the geographical conditions, etc. Then we do an evaluation based on corresponding principles for food therapy and select suitable functional food for prescriptions.

Bian zheng includes analyses of signs and symptoms collected through the four methods of diagnoses of observation, listening and smelling, inquiring, pulse and palpation in the light of the theory of TCM. Through it the doctor knows quite well about the cause, nature and location of a disease, as well as the relationship between pathogenic factors and the vital energy, and summarizing them into *zheng* of a certain nature (syndrome).

Generally speaking, the same syndromes are treated in similar ways, while different syndromes are treated in different ways. Take cold, exterior syndrome, for example (see Table 4).

Table 4　　Treating the Same Diseases with Different Methods

Exterior syndrome	Caused by wind-cold	Caused by wind-heat
manifestations	more severe chilliness, slight fever, a tongue with thin and white fur	more severe fever, milder chilliness, a tongue with thin and yellow fur
food for treatment	food pungent in taste and warm in property, to dispel the wind and cold	mild diaphoretic pungent in taste and cool in property, to dispel the wind and heat

This is called "treating the same diseases with different methods." Sometimes, different diseases have same syndromes in nature, so their treatments are basically the same. This is called "treating different diseases with the same method."

To summarize, the therapeutic aims are:

Twelve treatment principles

1) Excessive symptom-complexes should be treated by purgation and reduction.

2) Deficiency symptom-complexes should be treated with reinforcing or replenishing methods.

3) Cold symptom-complex should be treated with food or Chinese materia medica warm or hot in property.

42

4) Heat symptom-complex must be treated with food or Chinese materia medica cold in property.

5) External pathogenic factors must be removed. Sluggish flow of *qi* and blood must be treated with activating method.

6) Sluggish flow of *qi* and blood must be treated with activating method.

7) Dryness must be cured by moistening method.

8) Dampness must be removed.

9) Prolapse and ptosis must be treated with the lifting method.

10) Upward reversed action, e.g., cough, hiccough, must be suppressed.

11) What has become loose must be consolidated (e.g., nocturnal emission).

12) Debilitated and exhausted must be nourished (e.g., with warm-natured tonics).

3.2.3   The Theory of *Yin* and *Yang*

Yin and *yang* was originally included in the category of the ancient philosophy of China. At first, *yin* and *yang* describe whether a place faces the sun or not. The place being exposed to the sun is *yang*. Subsequently, through long periods of living, practice and observation of every kind of natural phenomenon, people realize that *yin* and *yang*, the two components which oppose each other, exist in all things. Furthermore, their interaction promotes the occurrence, development and transformation of things. As a consequence *yin* and *yang* are used to reason and analyze all the phenomena in the natural world.

The content of the theory of *yin* and *yang* can be described briefly as follows: opposition, interdependence, relative waxing and waning, and transformation.

By the opposition of *yin* and *yang*, we mean all things and phenomena in the natural world contain the two opposite attributes (see Fig. 6).

Fig. 6   **The Opposition of *Yin* and *Yang***

Yang		*Yin*
heaven	←——→	earth
outside	←——→	inside
functional movement	←——→	nourishing substance
movement	←——→	stability
going out	←——→	coming in
day	←——→	night
heat	←——→	cold
fire	←——→	water
upper side	←——→	lower side
rising	←——→	falling
rapid pulse	←——→	slow pulse
spring and summer	←——→	autumn and winter

These opposite pairs show that *yin* and *yang* exist within all things and phenomena.

Yin and *yang* not only oppose but also depend on each other, without the other, neither can exist. This relationship of coexistence is known as interdependence.

Yin and *yang* opposing each other and yet depending on each other for existence are not stagnant but dynamic, i.e., while *yin* wanes, *yang* waxes, and vice versa. This dynamic change of succeeding each other between *yin* and *yang* is known as the waxing and waning of *yin* and

44

yang.

By "transformation" we mean *yin* and *yang* will transform into each other under certain conditions.

The general principle for distinguishing between *yin* and *yang* is as demonstrated in Table 5.

Table 5   The General Principle for Distinguishing Between *Yin* and *Yang*

Yang	hyperfunctional, excited, hot, moving, strong, bright, invisible, light and clear, up and upwards, out and outward, dynamism, and all that have active specific characteristics belong to *yang*.
Yin	waning, restricted, cold, weak, dark, visible, heavy and turbid, down and downward, inside and inwards, quiescence, and all that have inactive specific characteristics belong to *yin*.

Therefore, *Basic Questions* states, "*Yin* and *yang* are the law of heaven and earth, the outline of every thing, the parents of all changes, the origin of birth and destruction, and the source of all mysteries."

It should be pointed out that the *yin* or *yang* property of things is not absolute but relative. This relativity of *yin* and *yang* is shown in the inter-transformation between *yin* and *yang* mentioned above, i.e., *yin* may transform into *yang* and vice versa; it is also shown in the constant divisibility of *yin* and *yang*, i.e., either *yin* or *yang* can be further divided into another pair of *yin* and *yang* (see Fig. 7).

Fig.7   The Constant Divisibility of *Yin* and *Yang*

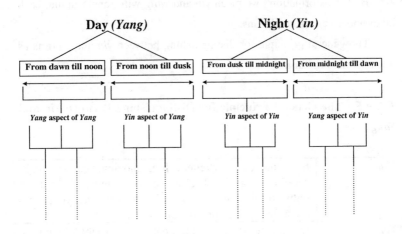

Day *(Yang)*   Night *(Yin)*

| From dawn till noon | From noon till dusk | From dusk till midnight | From midnight till dawn |

Yang aspect of *Yang*   *Yin* aspect of *Yang*   *Yin* aspect of *Yin*   *Yang* aspect of *Yin*

Yin and *yang* are used to explain the tissues and structures, physiology and pathology of the human body, and direct clinical diagnosis and treatment (see Table 6).

Table 6   *Yin* and *Yang* of the Human Body

Yang	Yin
Upper part Exterior back	lower part interior abdomen
the lateral aspect of the extremities	the medial aspect of the extremities
the six *fu*-organs (the gall-bladder, stomach, large intestine, small intestine, urinary bladder and *san-jiao*)	the five *zang*-organs (the heart, liver, spleen, lung and kidney)

The relationship between *yin* and *yang* also remains constant among the five viscera. The heart and lung are *yang*, because they are higher, while the liver, spleen and kidney are *yin*, because they are lower. When speaking of *yin* and *yang* of every organ, the function is *yang*, the substance *yin*.

TCM believes that the normal physiological functions of the human body result from the opposition, unity and coordinate relation between *yang* (function) and *yin* (substance). *Yin* and *yang* are always in the state of dynamic balance. It is known as: "*Yin* is even and well, while *yang* is firm, hence a relative equilibrium is maintained and health is guaranteed."

In TCM, it is thought that the imbalance of *yin* and *yang* is one of the basic pathogeneses of a disease.

In TCM, in making a diagnosis, the first important thing is to ascertain whether the disease is *yin* or *yang* (see Table 7).

Table 7 Application of the Theory of *Yin* and *Yang* in Making a Diagnosis

	Yang character	*Yin* character
In observation of the patients' complexion	look bright	look dark and gloomy
In listening and smelling	have a loud and clear voice	have a low and weak voice
In inquiring	have a fever	have an aversion to cold
	feel thirsty	don't feel thirsty
	suffer from constipation	have loose stools

In pulse feeling and palpation	have a rapid pulse condition	a slow pulse condition
	Floating	deep
	Rapid	slow
	large	small
	slippery	rough
	full	empty

The general property of food or Chinese materia medica are determined by their property, taste and their actions, such as ascending, floating, descending and sinking.

The property, taste and function of food or Chinese materia medica can also be summarized in the light of the *yin* and *yang* theory, and this forms a basis for the clinical application of food or Chinese materia medica (see Table 8).

Table 8   The Property, Taste and Function of Food or Chinese Materia Medica Can Also Be Summarized in the Light of the *Yin* and *Yang* Theory

	Yin	*Yang*
Property	cold and cool	warm and hot
Taste	sour, bitter and salty	pungent, sweet
Function	astringent and subsiding	dispersing, ascending and floating

In TCM, the principles of treatment are established on the basis of the predominance or weakness of *yin* and *yang*. Once the principle is established, herbs are selected according to their property of *yin* and *yang* and their function. By doing so, one can cure diseases.

3.2.4 Theory of Five Elements

According to the theory of the five elements, wood, fire, earth, metal and water are five basic substances that constitute the material world. In the beginning, the theory of five elements was probably based on some knowledge of natural physics, such as the ability of wood to produce fire, of water to extinguish fire, of fire to melt metals, of metal instrument to cut wood, of earth to produce metals, etc. It was further extended to explain the relationship of all things. These substances are not only related by generation and restriction but are set in a state of constant motion and change.

Among the five elements, there exist the relations of generation, restriction, subjugation and reverse restriction.

The order of generation, restriction relations among the five elements is as follows (see Fig. 8).

Fig. 8 Generation, Restriction Relations Among the Five Elements

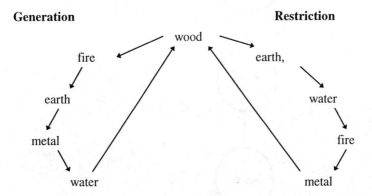

As far as the relationship of generation of each of the five elements is concerned, it is composed of two aspects – generating and being generated. The element that generates is called mother, while the element that is generated is called the son. Hence, the relation of generating and being generated among the five elements is also known as that of mother and son. Take wood for example. Because wood produces fire, it is called the mother of fire. On the other hand it is produced by water, so it is called the son of water.

Restriction connotes bringing under control or restraint. So far as the relationship of restriction that the five elements possess is concerned, it works in the following order (see Fig. 9).

Each of the five elements has the chance of restricting and being restricted. Take wood for example. The element restricting wood is metal, and the element that is restricted by wood is earth (see Fig. 10).

Fig. 9   The Restriction Relations of Related to Wood

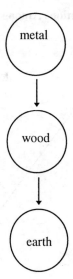

Without generation, there would be no birth and development; without restriction, excessive growth would result in harm.

Should one of the five elements be excessive or insufficient, there would appear the phenomena of abnormal restriction, known as subjugation and reverse restriction.

By subjugation is meant that one element subdues the other when the latter is weak. It is the manifestation of abnormal coordination among things. For instance, if wood is in excess and metal can not exercise normal restriction on it, then the excessive wood will subjugate earth in such a way that earth will become weaker (see Fig. 10).

Fig. 10   Restriction and Reversing Restriction Among the Five Elements

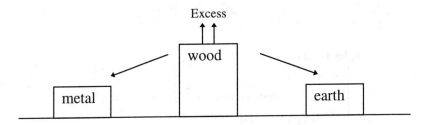

Reverse restriction means one preying upon the other. That is, when any one of the five elements is in excess, the one originally restricting it will be restricted by it instead. For instance, the normal order of restriction is that metal restricts wood; but if wood is in excess or metal is insufficient, wood will restrict metal in the reverse direction. It is clear that the order of reverse restriction is just opposite to that of restriction and that reverse restriction is undoubtedly a harmful one.

The generation of the five elements can be used to expound the

51

interdepending relations between the five viscera (see Fig. 11).

Fig. 11   The Interdepending Relations Between the Five Viscera

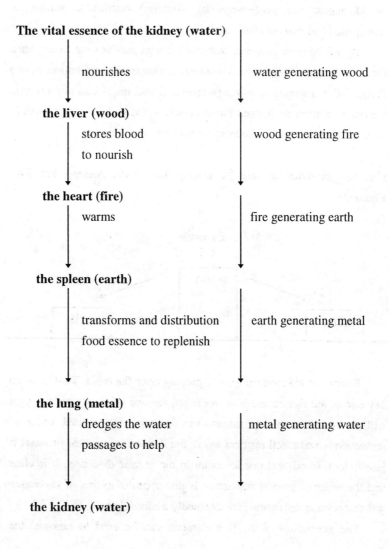

The vital essence of the kidney (water)

nourishes   water generating wood

the liver (wood)

stores blood   wood generating fire
to nourish

the heart (fire)

warms   fire generating earth

the spleen (earth)

transforms and distribution   earth generating metal
food essence to replenish

the lung (metal)

dredges the water   metal generating water
passages to help

the kidney (water)

The restriction of the five elements can be used to explain the inter-restraining relations between the five viscera (see Fig. 12).

Fig. 12   The Inter-restraining Relations Between the Five Viscera

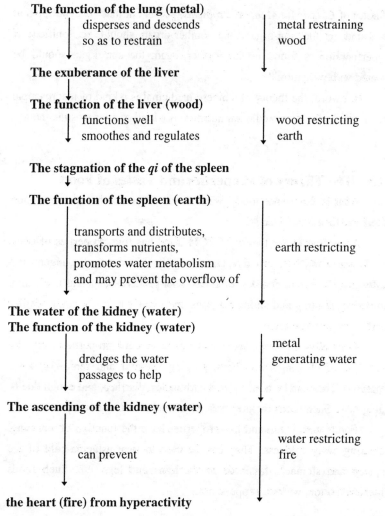

The function of the lung (metal)
disperses and descends   metal restraining
so as to restrain   wood

The exuberance of the liver

The function of the liver (wood)
functions well   wood restricting
smoothes and regulates   earth

The stagnation of the *qi* of the spleen

The function of the spleen (earth)

transports and distributes,
transforms nutrients,   earth restricting
promotes water metabolism
and may prevent the overflow of

The water of the kidney (water)
The function of the kidney (water)

metal
dredges the water   generating water
passages to help

The ascending of the kidney (water)

water restricting
can prevent   fire

the heart (fire) from hyperactivity

As the 77th Problem, a chapter of *Classic on Medical Problems* says, "When liver disease occurs, it will spread to the spleen, so the *qi* of the spleen should be reinforced before it is affected."

Also the theory of five elements may be used to help work out the principle and method of treatment. For instance, the 69th Problem, a chapter of *Classic on Medical Problems*, points out that "if hypofunction is found in the son-organ, the mother-organ should be tonified; if hyperfunction is found in the mother-organ, the son-organ should be treated with purgation."

In a word, the theory of Chinese medicinal is a kind of macroscopic theory while Western medicinal nutrition is a kind of microcosmic theory.

3.3   The Theory of Properties and Tastes of Food

What is functional food? What is the difference between common food and functional food?

According to the theory of TCM, food has four properties of cold, cool, warm and hot, and five tastes of sour, bitter, sweet, pungent and salty just like herbs. Besides, food has other properties, such as the lifting, lowering, floating and sinking actions, meridian's tropism, compatibility and so on just like herbs.

Generally speaking, foods with cold or cool properties have the function of clearing away heat, purging fire-evil and removing toxic material. They can be used to treat carbuncles, diarrhea, and cough due to lung-heat. Such foods include crab, bitter melon, mung bean, pear, etc.

Foods with warm and hot properties have the function of warming, clearing away coldness. They can be used to treat asthenia-cold of the spleen and stomach, lassitude in the loins and legs, etc. Such foods include mutton, walnut, peppers, etc.

Ordinary people can use foods with mild properties. These foods are carrot, an edible fungus, eggs, grapes, etc. (see Table 9).

Table 9   The Properties of Common Food

Properties	Common food
Cold	Wild rice stem, chrysanthemum, bitter melon, lotus root, crab, salt, sugarcane, tomato, water chestnut, kelp, orange peel, bamboo shoot, water melon, banana, cucumber, snail
Cool	Eggplant, towel gourd, millet, lettuce, white radish, rape, celery, millet, mung bean, bean curd, wheat, apple, pear, water melon peel, tea, pig' s skin, duck' s egg
Mild	Hyacinth bean, quail, seed of radish, sweet potato, potato, mushroom, cabbage, bean, carrot, black soy bean, red bean, yellow soy bean, corn, peanut, lily, sugar, lotus seed, black sesame, lotus leave, grape, pork, pig' s heart, pig' s kidney, turtle, honey, beef, milk
Warm	Silver carp, peach, fragrant-flowered garlic, ginger, Chinese onion, garlic, pumpkin, wine, vinegar, peach, cherry, black plum, litchi, chestnut, Chinese date, walnut, eel, lobster, carp, sea-cucumber, chicken, mutton, dog' s meat, pig's liver
Hot	Sweetbell red pepper, pepper

The five tastes refer to sour, bitter, sweet, pungent and salty. Foods with different tastes have different functions. For instance, foods with a sour taste have the function of contraction (see Table 10).

Table 10   The Tastes of Common Food

Sour	Plum, tomato, vinegar, red bean, pear, peach, Chinese hawthorn, orange, grape
Bitter	Bitter melon, wine, vinegar, lotus leave, tea, lily, pig's liver
Sweet	Chinese date, dried bean milk cream in tight rolls, mushroom, maize, soy bean
Pungent	Celery, ginger, Chinese onion, white radish, seed of radish, pepper
Salty	Three-colored amaranth, sea cucumber, salt, millet, kelp, crab, sea-cucumber, snail, pork, marrow, pig's kidney, pig's blood, dog's meat

If a patient suffers from abdominal pains and loose stools due to dyspepsia, what can we do? Chinese hawthorn, a fruit with sour taste can cure this disease. Fry Chinese hawthorn into coke and grind into fine powder. Take 9 grams, and add some brown sugar. Pour in boiling water, and mix. Consume when it is warm.

Foods with bitter taste can dry the wetness-evil, and clear away heat.

Foods with sweet taste have the functions of nourishing blood and *qi* and relieving convulsive disease.

The patient who suffers from weakness, anemia and neurasthenia can take mulberry syrup, which has a sweet taste. Take 10-15 grams each time, 2-3 times a day. Take it together with warm water or yellow wine.

Foods with a pungent taste have the function of dispersing exopathogens from surfaces of the body and regulating *qi* (vital energy) and relieving pain.

Foods with salty taste have the function of dissipating a mass, nourishing *yin* and suppressing *yang* (see Table 11).

Table 11   The Relationship Between the Five Tastes and Action

Taste	Act on	Action	Example
Sour	Liver	Astringent	Tomato, vinegar
Bitter	Heart	Antipyretic and moisture drying	Bitter melon, tea
Sweet	Spleen	Soothing and tonic	Chinese date, honey
Pungent	Lung	Dispersing and stimulating	White radish
Salty	Kidney	Purgative	Salt, kelp

Possibly some readers will ask questions such as, "You mentioned that watermelon has a cold property and bitter melon and pear have a cold property too. All of them have the same property – cold, but why do they have a different function? Why can they be used to treat different diseases? For example, watermelon can be used to clear away the heat in the stomach and heart. Pears are usually used to clear away the heat in the lung. Bitter melon can be used to treat the heat in the heart, for instance, palpitations due to heat, etc." My answer is that there was another theory in TCM. Certain foods pertain to certain meridians. This theory appeared in the Song Dynasty. It is used to select the sites on which the Chinese materia medica or food will act on.

Different tastes can go into different meridians. According to the theory of TCM, it is easy for sour taste to go into the liver and gall bladder.   It is easy for bitter taste to go into the heart and small intestine.

It is easy for sweet taste to go into the spleen and stomach. It is easy for a pungent taste to go into the lung and large intestine, and it is easy for a salty taste to go into the kidney and urinary bladder (see Table 12).

Table 12   The *Zang-Fu* Organs, Sites of Action of Common Food

Heart	Lotus roots, wine, tea, watermelon, sea-cucumber, mung bean, red bean, wheat, lotus leave, lily, longen, lotus seed, pig's skin, bitter melon
Liver	Tomato, vinegar, barbary wolfberry fruit, cherry, litchi, fragrant-flowered garlic, wine, vinegar, Chinese hawthorn, plum, black sesame, lobster, crab, lotus leave
Spleen	Ginger, eggplant, bean, chestnut, Chinese date, grape, honey, orange peels, mung beans, lotus root, tomato, bean curd, hyacinth bean, wild rice stem, carrot, sweet potato, garlic, millet, wheat, black soy bean, yellow soy bean, apple, peanut, watermelon peel, lotus leave, chestnut, grape, lotus seed, sugar, honey, pork, pig's liver, pig's blood, beef, chicken, mutton, dog's meat, eel, etc.
Lung	White radish, mushroom, peanut, sugarcane, banana, ginger, Chinese onion, garlic, carrot, celery, lily, pear, plum, orange, grape, walnut, pig's lung, duck's egg, orange peel, etc.
Kidney	Broad beans, small lobster, duck, Fleece-flower root, salt, black soybean, dried scallop, millet, wheat, sea-cucumber, eel, lobster, pork, pig's kidney, pig's marrow, quail's egg, mutton, dog's meat, pigeon's egg, black soy bean, sweet potato, cherry, black sesame, chestnut, grape, walnut, lotus seed, etc.
Stomach	Ginger, Chinese onion, bitter melon, lotus root, egg plant, tomato, white radish, bamboo shoot,

	cabbage, celery, cucumber, radish seed, potato, mushroom, bean, millet, mung bean, salt, bean curd, vinegar, sugarcane, apple, water chestnut, pear, peach, cheery, chestnut, Chinese date, milk, chicken, pork, pig' s stomach, beef, etc.
Bladder	Corn, snail, watermelon.
Large intestine	Potato, cabbage, bitter melon, egg plant, bean curd, bamboo shoot, soy bean, corn, plum, banana, honey, snail.
Small intestine	Salt, red bean, cucumber, sheep' milk.

After getting into the body, the food can go upwards or downwards based on its different properties.

Most of the thin in taste and light foods with the actions of lifting and floating have a pungent, sweet taste and warm or hot property. In contrast, most of the heavy foods with a strong taste and the actions of lowering and sinking have bitter, sour, salty taste and a cold or cool property.

The lifting, lowering, floating and sinking actions can also be altered through processing and combined use of foods. Take the crab as an example, the property of crab is cold and the taste is salty. So it is not good for the patient with weakness and cold constitution. What should they do if they want to eat crab? Do not worry about it. They can eat some food with the actions of lifting and floating and the properties of warm or hot together, such as ginger, Chinese onion, vinegar, wine, etc. In this way, the cold property of crab can be changed.

If you want to change the warm or hot property of peppers, you can add some food with a cold or cool property when you cook peppers, such as bitter melon. In this way, the hot property of pepper can be changed.

Besides, there is a funny theory in TCM. If one eats the kidney of an animal, it will reinforce his kidney; if a person eats a heart of an animal, it will reinforce his heart; if one eats a brain of an animal, it will nourish his brain.

Somebody asked me: "Who first determined the properties of food? How did he do it?"

Generally speaking, there were several methods to determine the properties of food in ancient China. The first was taste to see which property it has. For instance, watermelon has a cold property. In the second, doctor determined the properties of foods based on their effects. For instance, the doctor found that bananas could cause diarrhea. So he treated constipation with banana. In this way, we know the function and properties of banana. Take ginger as another example, if you have a pain in the stomach due to cold, after taking ginger soup, you will feel much better. So we can say, the property of ginger is hot or warm. That is to say, if the food can be used to treat a cold disease, we say it has a hot property.

In the case of a cold, many Western medical doctors would give you the same drugs – aspirin or something like that. But if you go to see Chinese doctors, after taking your pulse and looking at your tongue, etc., they would give you different herbal medicines. Maybe they would tell you that your diseases are different. One might say you suffer from wind-cold and another might say wind-heat. So for treating wind-cold, food with a warm property would be used, and for wind-heat, food with a cool property used.

To sum up, the theory of Chinese functional food is different from the theory of nutrition in Western medicine in two aspects:

(1) Western medical doctors pay more attention to the ingredients of food, such as the content of Vitamin C in orange juice or the content of protein in milk. People drink milk every day for protein. However Chinese medical doctors pay more attention to the properties of food, i.e.,

cold, hot, warm and cool properties.

(2) Chinese medical doctors prescribe for their patients a food recipe based on the different symptoms and syndromes or even different seasons, etc.

Chapter 4
Classification of Chinese Functional Food

There are several classifications of Chinese functional food. The classifications are based on the methods of preparation, main ingredients, or functions of the food, etc.

4.1 Classification According to the Preparation

Traditional Chinese functional food can be made in a variety of forms. The common forms are beverages, juices, soups, thick soups, porridge, cakes, instant drinks, spirits, honey syrups, preserved fruits or sweets, dishes, etc. Modern Chinese functional food can be made in some other forms apart from the traditional ones, for instance, extract, capsules, powder and even tablet (throat tablets), etc.

4.1.1 Beverages

Since ancient times, beverages have been used for administering medicine. They are usually prepared from light, thin-sliced materials, or from aromatic materials containing volatile compounds, which have been steeped in boiling or warm water.

The particular characteristic of beverages:

- They are not cooked but made in a similar way to tea.
- The most common raw material used in preparing beverages are flowers, leaves, fruits, peels, stems and twigs, and roots, and other substances which have been sliced thin or crushed.
- They can be taken like tea at any time during the day and in any quantity.

Common functional beverages are sweet ginger drink, vinegar-soaked ginger drink, green tea and honey drink, ginger and smoked plum tea, etc.

4.1.2 Juices

Fresh juices are prepared from succulent fruits, stalks, leaves, or root pieces, which have been pounded or squeezed. It is best to use them directly after preparation, without storage. If storage is required, first boil the juice in its container, seal tightly, and store in cold place to prevent fermentation.

Juices are usually taken as they are, but may also be mixed with water or wine. The amount and frequency of administration may depend on the patient's ability to take them.

Common functional juices are watermelon and tomato juice, sugarcane and lotus root juice, water chestnut juice, honeyed grape and ginger juice, white radish juice, potato juice, plum juice, pear juice, etc.

4.1.3 Soups

Soups are one of the oldest methods of administering medicines in TCM. Soups are easy to prepare. They are amenable to traditional medicine's dietetic treatment to suit individual needs. Their ingredients may be increased or reduced in quantity at will.

Soups are water bases for cooking Chinese medicine. In some cases, liquids such as spirits or vinegar can be added.

To make medicinal decoctions, we can cook herbs for a specific period of time, remove the liquid, and add more water to the sediment. Finally, the sediments are discarded and the liquids are mixed and taken. The herbs are generally cooked more than once. The medicinal herbs can be removed, and the infusion eaten along with edible ingredients. They can also be flavored with sugar or salt.

If very expensive herbs are used, or those that require much cooking, the soups can be steamed or stewed, e.g., stewing or steaming ginseng soup, etc.

Common functional soups are fermented beans, scallions, and rice wine soup, rice wine and mashed walnut soup, Chinese rose soup, ginseng lotus soup, etc.

4.1.4 Instant Drinks

Instant drinks become popular nowadays. The drinks are convenient, tasty and effective. Recently, many names have been given to instant drinks, such as "dried sugar," "instant tea," "instants," and "instant crystals." They are prepared and concentrated by cooking medicinal herbs or foodstuffs with juices. Enough powdered sugar is then added to form little grains. Finally, the grains are dried further. When needed, they can be easily reconstituted with boiling water.

Instant drinks are part of the traditional Chinese medicinal heritage. In order to suit household needs, the instant drink and their preparation have been slightly modified from their ancient forms.

There are other benefits of instant drinks. When the herbs or foods are in season or are easy to cook, an extra amount can be made for future use. Instant drinks can be stored for a long time without affecting their quality. Processing see Fig. 13.

Prepared instants can be stored in a tightly sealed glass jar.

Common functional instant drinks are instant lemonade, willow leaf instant (the best time to collect willow leaf is the days around April 5 or April 6 each year), corn silk instant, cucumber leaf instant, etc.

4.1.5 Spirits

Spirits and medicinal spirits have a long history. The oracle bones and turtle shells of the Shang periods contained the inscription: "鬯其酒" (spirits made from fragrant turmeric root). Publications on spirits have helped medicine, particularly pharmaceuticals and food therapy take a big step forward. In addition to the fact that alcoholic beverages allow the extraction of active ingredients from medicines which are difficult to extract by water, they have their own intrinsic therapeutic power. They have the effects of clearing blood vessels, nourishing vital energy in the spleen, enriching the intestines and stomach, moistening the skin, dispelling cold vapors, and enhancing the efficacy of medicines. Thus, the ancients had a saying that "spirits are the chief of all medicines."

There are three classes of medicinal spirits (see Table 13).

Table 13   Three Classes of Medicinal Spirits

Spirits	Alcoholic drinks with regular medicines
Sweet spirits	Having, in addition to regular medicines, sugar or very sweet medicines
Undecanted spirits	Having, in addition to regular medicines and sugar, the dregs or mash from which the spirits are remaining in the liquid

Brewing spirits is not difficult, and can be carried out in any household. Some simple methods are as follows:

Fig. 13   The Processing of Instant Drinks

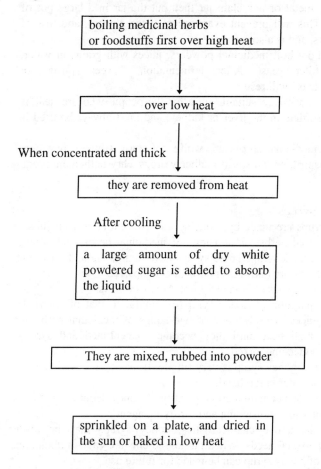

boiling medicinal herbs
or foodstuffs first over high heat

over low heat

When concentrated and thick

they are removed from heat

After cooling

a large amount of dry white powdered sugar is added to absorb the liquid

They are mixed, rubbed into powder

sprinkled on a plate, and dried in the sun or baked in low heat

Cold Soak Method: soak any amount of medicines in spirits of a particular proof. Shake often, and store for a specified period of time before using.

Hot Soak Method: first boil the medicines in spirits for a specified period of time, then let cool and store. This is an ancient method of preparing and using medicinal spirits. In the Han Dynasty, there was green plums boiled in spirits. This method will speed up and facilitate easy extraction of active ingredients. However, when boiling alcohol, one must be very careful to prevent fire. The best way is to put the medicines and spirits in a metal or porcelain jar then put the jar in a large pot of boiling water. This will prevent evaporation of the alcohol, and loss of effective powers, and is also safer.

Dreg Method: boil medicinal powders, juices with grains in water, then add distiller yeast. After fermentation, "sweet spirits" or "undecanted spirits" will result.

Medicinal spirits are suitable only for the people who are healthy without any disorders in the liver or kidney, and must always be used in moderation.

Common medicinal spirits are wolfberry spirit, Chinese hawthorn spirit, ginseng spirit, prawn spirit, mulberry dregs, chrysanthemum dregs, etc.

4.1.6 Honey Syrups

Honey syrups are made by reducing and concentrating fruit juices, juices of medicinal herbs, or infusions of medicinal herbs, and adding honey to form a thick syrup. These syrups have nourishing and fortifying properties, and thus are known as nourishing syrups.

The Characteristics of Honey Syrups Are as Follows:

* The preparation of honey syrups is similar to that of soups. In general, fruit juices or collections of two soups of medicinal herbs are cooked over small heat until they become concentrated and syrupy. Honey is then added and mixed.

* The use of honey syrup is very simple. It may be taken directly or dissolved in hot water beforehand.

* Honey syrups contain a great quantity of honey. Honey is not only a flavoring, but also a moistening and fortifying agent.

* With the above characteristics, honey syrups may be made according to personal needs. When the ingredients are easy to obtain, an extra amount of honey syrup can be made for future use.

* Honey syrups should be stored in a dark colored, wide-mouthed bottle, sealed tightly, and stored in a cool place away from light.

Common functional honey syrups are sesame oil syrup, mutton fat syrup, ginger syrup, mulberry syrup, grape and lotus root syrup, etc.

4.1.7 Porridge

Porridge is made from rice, millet, sorghum, barley, wheat and any other abundantly starchy grains. Functional porridge is usually made with the above mentioned ingredients with the addition of other nutritious foods, such as meat, fruits, or other Chinese materia medica.

Functional porridge has a long history in China. In the pre-Qin period, there is a record of an illness-curing millet soup.

The preparation of the porridge is simple. If edible ingredients such as jujube, chestnuts and walnuts are used, they can be cooked with the grains; inedible Chinese materia medica can be boiled alone first, and the strained liquid mixed in with the grains afterwards. The consumption of porridge is limited only by a person's appetite. If increased efficacy is desired, then the quantity or frequency of porridge consumed should also be increased.

Common functional porridges are black sesame porridge, walnut porridge, litchi porridge, pear porridge, spinach porridge, mung beans and cabbage porridge, eight-treasure porridge, etc.

4.1.8 Thick Soups

The main ingredients of thick soups are meats, eggs, milk or seafood. Thick soups can be eaten as the main dish or as an accompaniment.

Functional thick soups follow the same principles of any ordinary thick soup, but they are just made with tasty or bland medicinal substances. Thick soups are made just like soups. If the medicinal substances are edible, they can be cooked with the main ingredients directly. If the substances are not edible, the sediments and inedible parts can be removed. Alternatively, the substances can be wrapped in a cloth and added in with the main ingredients. Before eating, the medicine bundle can be removed.

Common functional soups are sugar and egg white soup, ginger, orange, pepper and fish soup, chicken's liver soup, pig's kidney soup, pig's liver soup, Chinese yam, milk and mutton soup, etc.

4.1.9 Candies

Candies are made of white sugar, rock sugar, brown sugar or malt sugar as the most important ingredients. They have been prepared by boiling with water to become solid or semi-solid, and can be sucked on or chewed. Many candies have fruit, condensed milk or fillings. There are many kinds of candies: hard, soft, creamy, crispy, filled candy, etc.

Functional candies are made by adding powders, juices or extracts of medicinal herbs that have been cooked with some form of sugar. In addition, cooked nuts or fruits can be added to cooked sugar.

This form of food can be made in any household. Because of the sweet taste, they can be given to children who do not like to take medicine. They can be eaten in any amount, and can be stored for a long time.

Common functional candies are persimmon powder candy, candy to aid digestion, mint candy, mulberry candy, longan and orange candy, peanut candy, walnut candy, pine nut candy, etc.

4.1.10 Honey Preserved and Sugared Fruit

Honey-preserved and sugared fruits are made from fresh fruits processed with honey or sugar. This category of food is sweet, tasty and refreshing, and can be eaten with meals or as snacks.

Functional preserved and sugared fruits are mostly made from plant fruits, peel, or fresh or dried medicinal herbs that have been cooked in medicinal extracts, honey, or sugar, and then cooked with more honey or sugar. They are not difficult to prepare; anyone could be able to make them. When the basic ingredients are in abundance, the extra should be made and stored for future use.

The characteristic of honey-preserved and sugared fruits:

* The color and taste of fresh food or medicinal herbs are preserved.

* Honey and white sugar fortify and soothe the stomach, quench dryness and stimulate salivation. They also have some antiseptic properties that enable these foods to be stored for long periods of time without altering quality.

* The medicinal herbs used in this kind of food have a sweet-bland flavor and are neutral.

* Usually, there is no limit to dosage. A person can take as much as he wants.

Common functional honey preserved and sugared fruits are honey-preserved haws, honey-preserved pears, honey-preserved cucumber, honey-preserved mulberries, honey-preserved radish, honey-preserved lily, sugared watermelon, sugared orange peel, sugared lemons, sugar-preserved flavored dates, etc.

4.1.11 Foods Made from Rice and Flour

Foods made from rice and flour use polished long-grained rice and polished glutinous rice and flour as the most important ingredient. These foods can be eaten as meals or as snacks. They have been prepared by steaming, boiling with water, frying with oil, baking in a pan or in an oven to make medicated cake, pancake, and dumpling, etc.

This form of food can be made in any household and eaten in any amount. It is best to use them directly after preparation. Usually, this kind of food cannot be stored for a long time.

Common functional pancakes that can benefit the spleen are lotus seed cake, broad bean cake, lotus and rice cake, chestnut cake, cooked rice and wheat flour, Chinese yam rice buns, etc.

4.1.12 Cooked Dishes

Cooked foods involve the preparation of vegetables, chicken, duck, fish, meat, shrimp, crab, eggs and other foods. Cooking is a complex art and the range of ingredients is broad; thus, there are many preparation methods, such as cold salads, stewing, stir-frying, boiling, deep-frying, quick-frying, steaming, quick boiling, and pickling.

In ancient China, food is as important as medicines. So there is a motto "use food to fortify the body." The most efficient cooked dishes used to cure and fortify contain appropriate medicinal herbs as the main ingredients.

Cooked dishes emphasize color, fragrance, taste, and shape. Thus, most functional dishes do not contain very much medicine. They can be eaten in any amount. Cooked dishes must use fresh ingredients. The freshly cooked dishes should be consumed immediately.

4.2 Classification According to the Main Ingredients

4.2.1 Grains: polished round-grained rice, millet, wheat, buckwheat, Chinese sorghum, seed of Job tears, maize, etc.

4.2.2 Beans: yellow soybean, bean curd, mung bean, black sesame, red bean, broad bean, etc.

4.2.3 Birds and animals: pork, pig's liver, pig's kidney, pig's skin, beef, mutton, dog meat, rabbit, black-bone chicken, chicken, duck, quail meat, edible bird nest, etc.

4.2.4 Aquatic products: carp, eel, turtle, crab, sea cucumber, frog, kelp, silver carp, dried scallop, shrimp, prawns, etc.

4.2.5 Egg and milk: quail egg, cow's milk, egg, duck egg, etc.

4.2.6 Vegetables: wax gourd, towel gourd, celery, spinach, garlic, Chinese yam, radish, carrot, lotus root, mushroom, tomato, eggplant, pumpkin, bitter melon, cucumber, fragrant-flowered garlic, lettuce, hyacinth bean, potato, etc.

4.2.7 **Fruits:** apple, banana, pear, peach, watermelon, grape, orange, Chinese hawthorn, Chinese date, sugarcane, water chestnut, mulberry, cherry, plum, litchi, etc.

4.2.8 **Nuts:** walnut, sweet almond, chestnut, pine nut, peanut, sunflower seed, etc.

4.2.9 **Condiments:** wine, salt, vinegar, thick sauce, peanut oil, pepper, honey, crystal sugar, green Chinese onion, ginger, green tea, etc.

4.2.10 **Chinese materia medica:** Arrillus Longan (Longyanrou), Cortex Cinnamomi (Rougui), Flos Chrysanthemi (Juhua), Folium Perillae (Zisuye), Fructus Amomi (Sharen), Fructus Aurantii (Daidaihua), Fructus Cannabis (Huomaren)

4.3 Classification According to the Functions

At present, the authorized institutes in China for testing functional food need to perform 24 tests on functional food products:

4.3.1 **Immune regulation: Hao Kang Main Yi Ye** (昊康免疫液), Zhong Hua Sheng Wu Shen (中华生物参), Gu Sui Zhuang Gu Fen (骨髓壮骨粉), etc.

4.3.2 **Postponement of senility:** Huang Bei Bao (皇贝宝), Shen Fu Jiu (神蚨酒), Sheng Wu Jian Kou Fu Ye (生物健口服液), etc.

4.3.3 **Memory improvement:** Sheng Ming Yi Hao (生命一号), Jin Gu Er Tong Kou Fu Ye (金菇儿童口服液), Nao Li Jian Kou Fu Ying Yang Ye (脑力健口服营养液), etc.

4.3.4 **Promotion of growth and development:** Jin De Fu He Gai 200 (劲得复合钙200), Qiang Li Pai Er Tong Ying Yang Ye (强力牌儿童营养液), Gui Feng Ying Yang Ye (龟凤营养液), etc.

4.3.5 **Anti-fatigue:** Bao Zhong Bao Gong Neng Ying Yang Yin Pin (宝中宝功能营养饮品), Hong Jing Tian Mi Pian (红景天蜜片), Xi Yue Yang Shen Kou Fu Ye (喜悦洋参口服液), etc.

4.3.6 **Body weight reduction:** Kang Er Shou Jian Fei Cha (康尔寿减肥茶), "Dan Jian" Jian Fei Ying Yang Pin ("丹健" 减肥营养品), Kang Mei Jian Fei Cha (康美减肥茶), etc.

4.3.7 **Oxygen deficit tolerance:** Miao Di Xue Geng (妙谛雪羹), Shen Hai Jiao Sha Xi (深海鲛鲨烯), etc.

4.3.8 **Radiation protection:** Zao Fu Kang (藻福康), Ke Li Kang Tian Ran Hu Luo Bu Su Kou Fu Ye (科力康天然胡萝卜素口服液), Bei Fang Pai Luo Xuan Zao Jiao Nang (北方牌螺旋藻胶囊), etc.

4.3.9 **Anti-mutation:** Hu Luo Bu Xian Zha Zhi (胡萝卜鲜榨汁), Jia Fu Lin Suan Jing Jiao Wan (I) (嘉福临蒜精胶丸(I)), Deng Kang Lu Kang Tu Bian Bao Jian Jiao Nang (登康路抗突变保健胶囊), etc.

4.3.10 **Anti-tumor:** Bu Wang Chong Cao Jing (补王虫草精), Wei Wang Pai Sha Yu Ruan Gu fen Jiao Nang (威望牌鲨鱼软骨粉胶囊), Fu Kang Jiao Nang (扶康胶囊), etc.

4.3.11 **Blood lipid regulation:** Li Zhi Jiang Zhi Cha (力芝降脂茶), Qiu Yuan Jiang Zhi Ye (秋源降脂液), Tong Ren Jiang Zhi Cha (同仁降脂茶), etc.

4.3.12 **Sex potency improvement:** Hai Dan Wang Pian (海胆王片), Li Bao Ye (利宝液), etc.

4.3.13 **Blood glucose regulation:** Rui Cao Tang An Kou Fu Ye (瑞草糖安口服液), Jian Wang Jiang Tang Nai Fen (健王降糖奶粉), A Er Fa Ying Yang Mian (阿尔发营养面), etc.

4.3.14 **Gastro-intestinal function improvement:** Jing Jing Bao Jian Yu Mi Fen (旌晶保健玉米粉), Ke Ni Na Xian Wei Su (科妮娜纤维素), Jin Chuan Bao Jian Pi Jiu (金川保健啤酒), etc.

4.3.15 **Sleep improvement:** Mei Le Su (Tui Hei Su) Pian (美乐素[褪黑素]片), Sai En Song Guo Ti Su Pian (赛恩松果体素片), Le Ning Jiao Nang (乐宁胶囊), etc.

4.3.16 **Improvement of nutritional anemia:** Bei Bei Xue Bao Er Tong Ying Yang Ye (贝贝血宝儿童营养液), Si Qiang Ru Suan Ying Yang Su (斯强乳酸营养素), etc.

4.3.17 **Protection of liver from chemical damages:** Jiu Lu Hui Kou Fu Ye (九鹿回口服液), An Tai Jiao Nang (安泰胶囊), Tai Kang Yi Gan Yin (泰康益肝饮), etc.

4.3.18 **Lactation improvement:** Yu Mu Li Sheng Ru Ling Jiao Nang (鱼牡蛎生乳灵胶囊), etc.

4.3.19 **Improvement for beauty:** Gei Ni Mei Kou Fu Ye (给你美口服液), Yi Mei Ting (伊美婷), Qi Cai Zhu Zhen Zhu Ye (七彩珠珍珠液), etc.

4.3.20 **Vision improvement:** Kang Shi Ming Kou Fu Ye (康视明口服液), Shi Li 1+1 (视力1+1), etc.

4.3.21 **Promotion of lead removal:** Qian Guo Hua Jiang Qian Bao Jian Ye (千果花降铅保健液),

4.3.22 **Removal of "intense heat" from the throat and moistening of the throat:** Cao Shan Hu Run Hou Tang (草珊瑚润喉糖), etc.

4.3.23 **Blood pressure regulation:** Jiang Ya Shen Cha (降压神茶), etc.

4.3.24 **Enhancement of bone calcification:** Wu Er Zhuang Gu Fen (武二壮骨粉), Ge Lin Gao Dan Bai Ying Yang Fen (格林高蛋白营养粉), Gu ying Yang Su Pian (骨营养素片), etc.

There are some other functions according to the theory of TCM, for instance, the functional food good for invigorating *qi*, nourishing the blood, nourishing *yin*, restoring *yang*, strengthening the spleen, tonifying the lung, nourishing the heart, tonifying the kidney, benefiting the liver and prolonging life, etc.

4.4 Classification According to the Indications

4.4.1 **Functional Food for Internal Diseases**, for instance, the functional food good for the patients with a cold or influenza, cough, bronchial asthma, stomach-ache, vomiting, indigestion, constipation, diarrhea, dysentery, hepatitis, icterus, edema, ascites, stranguria, nephritis, diabetes mellitus, coronary heart disease, hypertension, apoplexy, parasitosis, malarial disease, neurasthenia, palpitation, insomnia, seminal emission, impotence, premature ejaculation, etc.

4.4.2 Functional Food for Surgical Diseases, for instance, the functional food good for the patients of external diseases, scrofula, hemorrhoids, anal fistula, parotitis, frostbite, burn, scald, traumatic injury, bites or stings by insects, snakes or animals, etc.

4.4.3 Functional Food for Dermatological Diseases, for instance, the functional food good for the patients of proriasis, tinea, urticaria, eczematosis, etc.

4.4.4 Functional Food for Gynecological Diseases, for instance, the functional food good for the patients of dysmenorrhea, menorrhagia, metrorrhagia and metrostaxis, morbid leukorrhea, hyperemesis gravidarum, threatened abortion, hypogalactia, etc.

4.4.5 Functional Food for Children Diseases, for instance, the functional food good for the patients of pertussis, measles, diarrhea in children, maldigestion in children, rickets in children, bed-wetting in children, etc.

4.4.6 Functional Food for ENT Diseases and Ophthalmological Diseases, for instance, the functional food good for the patients of ophthalmological diseases, nasal diseases, diseases of mouth cavity, throat diseases, ear diseases, etc.

4.4.7 Functional Food with Auxiliary Curative Effect for Tumor, for instance, the functional foods good for the patients of nasopharyngeal carcinoma, thyroid cancer, mammary cancer, pulmonary carcinoma, liver cancer, carcinoma of esophagus, carcinoma of stomach, intestinal cancer, anus cancer, carcinoma of uterus, leukemia, etc.

4.5 Classification According to the Consumers

Chinese functional food can be classified into and fast or street food and imperial functional food according to different consumers.

4.5.1 Fast or Street Food

Generally speaking, fast food is a kind of "street food," which has been defined by the Food and Agriculture Organization (FAO) as "ready-to-eat foods and beverages prepared and/or sold by vendors especially in streets and other public places" (FAO, 1989).

With rapid urbanization, the demand for fast and street food has increased. The relationship between fast and street food and health is attracting more and more attention from the nutritionists of the world.

Take the fast food in Beijing as an example. Beijing is the capital of China. During recent years, with the population expansion, the quantity of fast and street foods has increased very quickly in the city.

Fast and street food business in Beijing provides jobs to many people. Millions of Beijing citizens consume fast and street food everyday. Consequently, they have a close relationship with the public's health. Bearing this in mind, I carried out studies on fast and street food in Beijing.

4.5.1.1 Fast and Street Food in Beijing – the Need of Fast-Paced Life-Styles

In the past, families in Beijing would dine together two or three times a day. But this picture has changed. More people are adopting the modern way of "fast living," which may be having a great impact on their eating behavior. Time is precious, and many people in Beijing are too busy to have regular meals. They hurry off in the morning without breakfast at home, then eat a pancake and a bowl of soybean milk on the street. Many of them grab a bowl of noodles at a fast-food stand instead of having formal lunch. In addition, because fast or street food is quick and easy to serve, it is often the choice of people who live alone or do not have the skill to cook for themselves. In Beijing, most young parents are employed, and they do not have time to buy and prepare food. As a result, the family may rely heavily on fast, quick and easy foods. Dinner may not be big because most people cannot afford to plan and shop carefully and prepare a balanced meal. So food preparation outside of the home by food service establishments and food manufacturers has replaced a large amount of food prepared at home. I think, that is the reason why fast and street foods are very popular in Beijing nowadays. And snacking has replaced regular meals in some families. People may also need a snack in the evening while they watch TV.

74

4.5.1.2 Classification of Fast and Street Food in Beijing

Fast food and street food in Beijing fall into three types:

1) Traditional fast and street food in Beijing.

The typical traditional fast food and street food in Beijing, such as millet paste (Chatang), are very famous. The millet paste is made by pouring boiling water into roasted millet powder with sugar. It tastes sweet and delicious. There are several kinds of ingredients for Chatang, and you can choose any one you like.

People in Beijing like thick soup of Doufu, a kind of jellied bean curd (Doufu Nao) very much. Every morning, after doing some physical exercises, they usually eat it with fried oil pancake (Zha You Bing) together for breakfast.

There are some other traditional fast and street foods in Beijing, for instance, black rice porridge (Zi Mi Zhou), glutinous rice cake (Lu Da Gun-er), rice cake (Ai Wo Wo), cake with nuts (Bai Guo Qie Gao), cake prepared in basin (Pen Gao), sweet Chinese hawthorn (Bing Tang Hu Lu), roast sweet potato (Kao Bai Shu), fried spring roll with oil (Zha Chun Juan), fried milk-cake with oil (Nai You Zha Gao), boiling pancake with pig's organs soup (Lu Zhu Huo Shao), vegetable or meat pie (Xian-er Bing), boiling pig's stomach quickly (Bao Du), fried noodles (Chao Mian), fried eggs with flour paste (Ji Dan Mi Wo), fried dumpling with oil (Jian Jiao Zi), boiling corn (Shui Zhu Yu Mi), spring pancake with roast beef (Chun Bing Kao Rou), fried starch with oil (Zha Guan Chang), pancake with sesame (Zhi Ma Huo Shao), big pancake (Da Bing), fried chestnut with sugar (Tang Chao Lizi), cold jellied mung bean (Liang Fen-er), etc.

2) Fast and street food from the other provinces or cities in China.

The people outside Beijing have brought many local foods to Beijing, for instance, fried cake with eight treasures (Ba Bao Su), fried flour roll (Zha Ma Hua), pancake (Lao Bing), pancake of corn (Tan Bing), fried dumpling (Guo Tie), thin pancake with eggs (Jian Bing), dishes with cabbage, carrot and other vegetables (Chao Cai), fried snail (Zha Luo Shi), sweet rice cake (Mi Tuan), steamed buns with meat fillings (Bao Zi), fried pancake with oil (Zha You Bing) and fried lotus root with meat inside (Zha Ou He), fried quail eggs (Zha An Chun Dan), fried lobster (Zha Long Xia), fried mutton in oil (Zha Yang Rou Chuan), etc. from Tianjin City; roast mutton (Kao Yang Rou Chuan) from Xinjiang Autonomous Region; noodle of rice/flour (Shaan Xi Niang Pi), pancake in mutton soup (Yang Rou Pao Mo), pancake with pork (Rou Jia

Mo) from Shaanxi Province; willow-like noodle made by a special knife (Dao Xiao Mian) from Shanxi Province; fried "Liang Fen-er," chafing dish of Chongqing and Dan Dan noodle, a spicy and hot dish, from Sichuan Province; pancake with green Chinese onion (Da Cong Jian Bing) and pancake with vegetable and meat stuffing (Da Lian Xian-er Bing) from Shandong Province; corn pancake (Tie Bing Zi) from northeast China; sticky rice cake (Zong Zi) from Fujian Province; fried steamed buns with meat fillings (Shui Jian Bao) from Shanghai, and so on.

3) Fast and street food from foreign countries.

In recent years, McDonald's, KFC, Pizza Hut and other foreign fast food restaurants have been swarming to Beijing. In the world-famous shopping area, Wangfujing, one cannot fail to recognize the biggest McDonald's in the world. KFC has also set up 100 stores in China. Fast and street foods from foreign countries, e.g., Thailand fried rice, Japanese Sapporo noodle and Korean cold noodle, are ready to make fast and street food market more competitive.

4.5.1.3　Fast and Street Food in Beijing – Part of Healthy Nourishment

With the improvement of living conditions, the demand for food is growing rapidly. In the past, people needed food because of hunger and coldness. Nowadays, however, they pay more attention to nutrition. Especially in the past 10 years, there have been great changes in people's daily food in Beijing. More and more people today come to realize the importance of health and the relationship between food and health.

The essential nutrients are categorized as fats, proteins, carbohydrates (sugars and starches), minerals, vitamins and water. They are called essential nutrients because we would become sick without them. We need them for energy, for building and maintaining body tissue, and for regulating body processes – the three essential functions of food in the body.

The ingredients used in fast and street food in Beijing, according to food classification, can be divided into groups as follows:

1) Meat: pork, mutton, pig's organs, sheep's organs, beef, chicken, quail, etc.

2) Seafood: fish, lobster, shrimp, prawn, snail, sea cucumber, etc.

3) Grain and beans: rice, black rice, glutinous rice, flour, millet, corn, mung bean, soybean, red bean, etc.

4) Vegetable: lotus root, carrot, mung bean sprout, garlic, green Chinese onion, celery, sweet potato, Chinese yam, cabbage, red-pepper, fragrant-flowered garlic, cucumber, tomato, bamboo shoot, etc.

5) Fruit: grape, Chinese hawthorn, orange, watermelon, Chinese date, pineapple, etc.

6) Nuts and seeds: walnut, sesame, lotus seed, watermelon seed, peanut, chestnut, etc.

7) Milk and eggs.

8) Chinese tea and other beverages.

From the foods mentioned above we can see that we can obtain all of the essential nutrients from fast and street food in Beijing.

Typical fast food and street food in Beijing include menus of fried mutton or fried oil pancake and soybean milk containing relatively high calories. However, their nutritional value in most other respects has been found to be reasonably good. It is a mistake to consider these foods, which are so popular with teenagers and young adults, worthless.

4.5.1.4   The Characteristics and Problems of Fast and Street Food in Beijing

About 20-30 years ago, there were few fast and street foods in Beijing. During recent years, Beijing has undergone great changes. In Beijing, the urban population has increased from 3 million in 1950 to the present 13 million. This was accompanied by an increase in the number of fast and street food vending establishments.

The characteristics of fast and street food in Beijing are as follows:

1) A choice for the public.

If you ask the people in Beijing whether they have tasted Chinese imperial meals in Fangshan Restaurant, 80 percent people would say, "No." However, you may find that all of them eat fast and street food in Beijing quite often. In fact, it is impossible for them to get away from fast and street food in their daily life.

2) Saving time.

There are fast or street food stands almost everywhere in Beijing. It is easy to find them.

3) Inexpensive.

The fast or street food in Beijing is quite cheap. The usual price is about 50 cents to one yuan for each serving. This price is acceptable for people with an average income.

4) Great variety, good taste and important source of nutrition.

There are many kinds of fast and street foods in Beijing with different tastes. Consumers can get a variety of fast food or street food which almost cover most daily food. It is clear that fast and street foods in Beijing are an important source of nutrition.

5) Convenient take-away.

It is convenient to take fast or street food away, for instance, pancake, roast mutton, dumpling, roast potato, etc. Hence, people usually buy some fast or street food on their way home from work.

6) Rich cultural and tourist attraction.

Beijing is famous for its long history as the center of Chinese cultural and political accomplishments. Its rich old traditions, precious cultural relics and historic sites have granted the city with peerless charms. Tourists can understand social customs and peculiar features of life through the fast and street food in Beijing. Let's take "Chatang" as an example, the skillful operation of the cook with the big copper pot is spectacular.

Every coin has two sides. Administration of fast or street food in Beijing has many problems, for instance, lack of adequate attention to issues of food safety, unhygienic or improper food preparation or handling practices, inappropriate locations for environmental reasons or causing traffic congestion, and poor personal habits or health of food handlers. Plates, glasses, spoons and other utensils are sometimes washed in a small container due to lack of basic facilities including running water. Chairs and tables offered to customers may not necessarily come up to safety standards and, in the evening, lighting may be provided through improvised wiring systems. All of these make up some problems associated with fast and street food vending in Beijing. The main reason is that the individual vendors who are directly involved in various operational activities, are not well educated, and know nothing about nutrition or basic hygiene. Consequently, the education and training of fast and street food vendors is as important as that of educating the public with regard to healthy lifestyles and eating habits.

4.5.2 Chinese Imperial Food

Chinese emperors lived in the imperial palace. They had special food for their special position. The imperial palace is named the Museum Palace (or Forbidden City), the former imperial palace. It is situated in the city's center and was the imperial palace of the Ming and Qing dynasties. (The palace was started in 1420, the Ming Dynasty, and the whole project occupied more than 720,000 square meters. It is now the biggest and the most intact ancient palace group in the country and even in the world.)

One of China's most famous classical gardens, the Summer Palace is situated in northwestern Beijing. Formerly an imperial garden and palace for the Qing emperor, it was first built by Qianlong, the fourth emperor of Qing Dynasty and was reconstructed in 1903. The Summer Palace is the largest and the best preserved of all extant imperil gardens in China. (The two main components of the garden are the Hill of Longevity and the Kunming Lake.) From the above we can see that the Chinese emperors' living conditions were quite different from their subjects. The tableware used daily and even the food containers were made from gold, gold bowls, gold dishes, gold chopsticks and gold spoons. However, was there any difference between street food or common food and imperial food? Actually, some famous Chinese imperial foods come from street food. Let's take pea cake and bean rolls as an example. It is said that one day Empress Dowager was cooling off in Jingxin Hall (静心殿), Summer Palace, when suddenly she heard somebody striking a gong in the street. She asked, "Who is striking the gong?" It was reported that someone was selling pea cakes and bean rolls. Empress Dowager was curious and summoned the man. Then the man presented the desserts to Empress Dowager. Tasting the sweet pea cakes and bean rolls, she found them delicious. The man was then ordered to work in the imperial kitchen to prepare these desserts for Empress Dowager.

Mimi-Wowotou is another example. Empress Dowager fled to Xi'an in panic when the Eight-Power Allied Forces occupied Beijing in 1900. One day on her way to Xi'an, she was extremely hungry. An ordinary peasant presented Wowotou (steamed corn flour bread) to her. She found it very delicious. When she returned to Beijing from Xi'an, she was reminded of the Wowotou and ordered the imperial cook to steam some for her. The chief of the imperial kitchen dared not steam big ones. Instead, he made a small and pretty type of Wowotou mixed much sugar and offered it to Empress Dowager. That was the history of Mimi-Wowotou. It was said that the Mimi-Wowotou was made of chestnut. But according to the chiefs in the imperial kitchen of the Qing Dynasty, Mimi-Wowotou was made of fine ground corn and sugar. Because it was so sweet people considered it to be chestnut Wowotou.

Some famous Chinese imperial foods come from common food that the emperor liked. For instance, Sesame Seed Cake with Minced Pork. It is told that one night Empress Dowager had a dream about eating sesame seed cake with minced pork. When she took breakfast the next morning, she found that one of the foods served was the sesame seed cake with minced pork that she dreamt of. Very happy, she said, "My dream has really come true." And she asked who made the cake. She was told that it was a cook named Zhao Yongshou. She granted Zhao a reward of 20 taels of silver. Since then sesame seed cakes with minced pork have become famous and popular.

Beihai Park is near the Forbidden City. The emperor and his family took it as their private park. Behind it in Beihai Park there is a famous restaurant for imperial dishes named Fangshan Restaurant.

Some Chinese imperial foods in the Qing Dynasty are functional foods, for instance, Stewed Bird's Nest（扒燕脯）, Braised Deer's Innards（烩全鹿）, Shark's Fin with Pigeon Eggs（凤尾鱼翅）, Braised Sea Cucumbers with Scallion（葱烧海参）, Jasmine with White Fungi（茉莉银耳）, Chicken Breast with Lotus Blooms（荷花鸡片）, Duck with Sesame（芝麻鸭子）, Diced Chicken with Fresh Lotus Seeds（鲜莲子鸡丁）, etc.

Roasted Sheep Heart with Rose (玫瑰花烤羊心), Soft Extract of "Jade" (琼玉膏), Soup of Sheep Viscera (羊脏羹) and Noodles of Pueraria Root Powder (葛粉羹), Noodles with Chinese Yam (山药面) are famous traditional Chinese imperial functional foods in the Yuan Dynasty.

Chapter 5
Food-and-Medicines Approved in China

5.1 Agkistrodon (蝮蛇, Fushe)

Pallas Pit Viper

Pallas pit viper is the dried body of *Agkistrodon halys* (Pallas) (Fam. Laminariaceae). It is collected in summer and autumn, opened in the abdomen or opened after the skin is stripped except the head and tail skin, removed from the viscera, coiled up in disc-shape and dried.

Chemical constituents: Arginine; phenylalanine; tyrosine; isoleucine; glutamic acid; threonine.

Pharmacological action: Its proteins showed anti-clotting and anti-cancer action.

Attributes: It is sweet in taste and warm in property. Acts on liver meridian.

Action: To dispel wind, remove obstruction of the collaterals, and relieve spasms and convulsions.

Indications: Chronic rheumatiod arthritis with numbness and ankylosis; hemiplegia in stroke; convulsions, tetanus, leprosy, scabies, scrofula with suppuration.

Dosage: 9-12g.

Storage: Preserve in a dry place, protected from mould and moth.

5.2 Arillus Longan (龙眼肉, Longyanrou)

Longan Aril

Longan aril is the aril of *Dimocarpus longan* Lour (Fam. Sapindaceae). It is collected in summer and autumn when the fruit is ripe, dried, removed from the shell and the nutlet, dried in the sun until it becomes unsticky.

Chemical constituents: Vitamin B_1, B_2, P, C; glucose, 2-amino-4-methyl-hex-5-ynoic acid, 2-amino-4-hydromethyl-hex-5-ynoic acid, and 2-amino-4-methyl-hept-6-ynoic acid

Pharmacological action: Its decoction showed inhibitory action against Microsporum audouini in vitro.

Attributes: It is sweet in taste and warm in property. Acts on heart and spleen meridians.

Action: To tonify the heart and the spleen, to nourish blood, and to tranquilize the mind.

Indications: Cardica palpitation, forgetfulness and insomnia due to deficiency of *qi* and blood; anemia.

Dosage: 9-15 g.

Storage: Preserve in a ventilated dry place, protected from moisture and moth.

5.3 Bulbus Allii Macrostemi (薤白, Xiebai)

Longstamen Onion Bulb

Longstamen onion bulb is the dried bulb of *Allium macrostemon* Bge (Fam. Liliaceae). It is collected in summer and autumn, washed clean, separated from its fibrous root, steamed thoroughly or scalded thoroughly in boiling water, and dried in the sun.

Chemical constituents:

1. Volatile oils: dimethyl-disulfide, 2,4-dimethyl-thiophene, methyl-allyl-disulfide, dimethyl trisulfide, methyl-allyl-trisulfide, propyl-allyl-trisulfide, methyl-propyl-disulfide, n-propyl-allyl disulfide.

2. Steroid saponins: macrostemonoside A, D, E, F, J, K, L; smilagenin-3-O-α-D-glucopyranosyl-(1-2)-β-D-galactopyranoside.

3. Others: postaglandin A_1 (PGA$_1$), B_1 (PGB$_1$), β-stigmasterol, carotene, succinic acid and adenosine.

Pharmacological action: The decoction had inhibitory action against Shigella dysenteriae and Staphylococcus aureus in vitro.

Attributes: It is pungent and bitter in taste and warm in property. Acts on lung, stomach and large intestine meridians.

Action: To remove the retained phlegm from the chest, promote the flow of *qi* and relieve its stagnation.

Indications: Angina pectoris; cough and dyspnea caused by retained phlegm; tenesmus in dysentery.

Dosage: 4.5-9 g.

Storage: Preserve in a dry place, protected from moth.

5.4 Bulbus Lilii (百合, Baihe)

Lily Bulb

Lily bulb is the dried fleshy scale leaf of *Lilium lancifolium* Thunb., *Lilium brownii* F. E. Brown *var. Viridulum* Baker or *Lilium pumilum* DC.(Fam. Liliaceae). It is collected in autumn, washed clean, heated with boiling water briefly, and dried.

Chemical constituents:

1. Glycerides: 2,3-dihydroxy-3-O-ρ-coumaroyl-1,2-propanedicarbo-xylic acid; 1,3-O- diferuloylglycerol; 1,2-O-diferuloylglycerol; 1-O-feruloyl-3-O-p-coumaroylglycerol; 1-O-feruloyl-2-O-ρ-coumaroylgly-cerol; 1-O-ρ-coumaroyl-2-O-feruloylglycerol; 1-O-feruloylglycerol; 1-O-ρ-coumaroyl-glycerol.

2. Phenolic glycosdies: regaloside A, B, C, D, E, F; regaloside.

3. Steroid glycosides: (22S, 25S)-26-O-β-D-glucopyranosyl-22, 25-epoxyfurost-5-en-3β-26-diol 3-O-(α-L-rhamnopyranosyl-(1-2)-β-D-glu-copyranoside; 26-O-β-D-glucopyranosylnuatigenin-3-O-α-L-rhamno-pyranosyl-(1-2)-β-D-glucopyranoside; 26-O-β-D-glucopyranosy-lnuatigenin-3-O-α-L-rhamnopyranosyl-(1-2)-(β-D-glucopyranosyl-(1-4))-β-D-glucopyranoside; 27-O-(3-hydroxy-3-methylglutaroyl)-isonarthao-genin-3-O-α-L-rhamnopyranosyl-(1-2)-(β-D-glucoyranosyl-(1-4))-β-D-glucopyranoside.

4. Others: meconic acid; β-solamargine; solasodine-3-O-α-L-rhamnopyranosyl-(1-2)-O-(β-D- glucopyranosyl-(1-4))- β-D-glucopyra-noside.

Pharmacological action: Its decoction can relieve the cough induced by ammonia in mice.

Attributes: It is pungent and bitter in taste and warm in property. Acts on heart and lung meridians.

Action: To nourish yin and moisten the lung, and to tranquilize the mind.

Indications: Deficiency of yin with chronic cough and bloody sputum;fidgetiness, palpitation, insomnia, Dream disturbed sleep and absent-mindedness.

Dosage: 6-12 g.

Storage: Preserve in a dry place.

5.5 Concha Ostreae (牡蛎, Muli)

Oyster Shell

Oyster shell is the shell of *Ostrea gigas* Thunberg, *Ostrea talienwhanensis* Crosse or *Ostrea rivularis* Gould (Fam. Osteridae). It is collected all the year round, removed from soft part, washed clean, and dried in the sun.

Chemical constituents: $NaCO_3$, $CaSO_4$, $Ca_3(PO_4)_2$, Na, Bi, Al, Mn, Zi, Si, Cu and Mg.

Pharmacological action: Its extract inhibits the growth of poliovirus in vivo.

Attributes: It is salty in taste and slightly cold in property. Acts on liver, gall-bladder and kidney meridians.

Action: To nourish *yin* and subdue the overflowing of *yang*, to induce sedation, to soften hard masses and eliminate nodulation, and to arrest discharges.

Indications: Palpitaton, insomnia, dizziness and tinnitus; scrofula, mal formation in the abdomen; spontaneous sweating and night sweating; seminal emission; abnormal uterine bleeding, excessive leukorrhea; epigastric pain with acid regurgitation.

Dosage: 9-30 g.

Storage: Preserve in a dry place.

5. 6 Cortex Cinnamomi (肉桂，Rougui)

Cassia Bark

Cassia bark is the dried stem bark of *Cinnamomum cassia* Presl (Fam. Lauraceae). It is frequently collected in autumn, and dried in the shade.

Chemical constituents:

1. Volatile oils: cinnamic aldehyde, cinnamyl alcohol, cinnamyl acetate, cinnamic acid, phenylpropyl acetate and coumarin.

2. Polysaccharides: cinnaman AX.

3. Sesquiterpenoids: cassiol, cassioside and cinnamoside.

4. Diterpenoids: cinnzeylanine; cinnzeylanol; cinnacassiol A; cinnacassiol A-19-O-β-D-glucopyranoside; cinnacassiol B; cinnacassiol B-19-O-β-D-glucopyranoside; cinnacassiol C_1; cinnacassiol C_2; C_3; anhydrocinnzeylanine, cinnzeylanol; cinnacassiol D_1, D_2, D_3 and E.

5. Flavanoids: (-)-epicatechin; (-)-epicatechin-3-O-β-D-glucopyranoside; procyanidin B_2; 8-C-glucopyranosyl-procyanidin; 6-C-β-D-glucopyranosyl-procyanidin B_2; procyanidin B_1, B_5, B_7; proanthocyanidin A_2, C_1; 6-C-β-D-glucopyranosyl-epicatechin; 8-C-glucopyranosyl-(-)-epicatechin; cinnamtannin A_2, A_3, A_4.

6. Others: protocatechuic acid; syringic acid; biotin; 3-(2-hydroxypheneyl)-propanoic acid; 3,4,5-trimethoxyphenyl-β-D-apiofuranosyl- (1-6)- β-D-glucopyranoside.

Pharmacological action: Cinnamic oil contains cinnamic aldehyde, cinnamic acid and cinnamyl acetate and is an aromatic stomachic and carminative. It weakly stimulates the gastrointestinal tract, promotes salivary and gastric secretion and strengthens the digestive action. It also relieves spasms of the smooth muscle of internal organs and relieves pain due to intestinal spasms. Its decoction increases coronary flow in the isolated heart of guinea pigs and partially antagonizes pituitrin in reducing the coronary flow. The decoction has an inhibitory action against fungi in vitro.

Attributes: It is pungent and sweet in taste and hot in property. Acts on kidney, spleen, heart and liver meridians.

Action: To supplement body fire, reinforce *yang*, and lead the fire back to the kidney, to dispel cold and relieve pain, and to activate blood circulation and stimulate menstrual discharge.

Indications: Impotence, frigidity, feeling of coldness and pain in the loins and knees; dyspnea in deficiency syndrome of the kidney; dizziness, inflammation of the eye and sore throat due to *yang* deficiency; precordial and abdominal pain with cold sensation, vomiting and diarrhea in deficiency-cold syndromes; neurosis with a feeling of gas rushing up through the chest to the throat from the lower abdomen; a-menorrhea, dymenorrhea.

Dosage: 1-4.5 g.

Storage: Preserve in well-sealed containers, stored in a cool and dry place.

5.7 Endothelium Corneum Gigeriae Galli (鸡内金, Jineijin)

Chicken's Gizzard-Skin

Chicken's gizzard-skin is the dried inner wall of the gizzard of *Gallus gallus domesticus* Brisson (Fam. Phasianidae). The gizzard is collected after the chicken is killed. The inner wall of the gizzard is peeled off immediately, washed clean, and dried.

Pharmacological action: Its powder can increase the secretion and lower the pH of gastric juice.

Chemical constituents: Proteins, Al, Ca, Cu, Fe, Vitamin B_1, B_2, C.

Attributes: It is sweet in taste and mild in property. Acts on spleen, stomach, small intestine and bladder meridians.

Action: To promote digestion, to arrest seminal emission, and to cure enuresis.

Indications: Vomiting and diarrhea due to indigestion, malnutrition due to improper feeding, and enuresis in children; seminal emission.

Dosage: 3-9g.

Storage: Preserve in a dry place, protected from moth.

5.8 Exocarpium Citri Rubrum (橘红， Juhong)

Red Tangerine Peel

Red tangerine peel is the dried exocarp of *Citrus reticulata* Blanca and its cultivars (Fam. Rutaceae). The ripe fruit is collected in late autumn and early winter, the exocarp is peeled and collected, dried in the sun or in the shade.

Chemical constituents: Hesperidin, neohesperidin, Vitamin C, cyptoxanthin, tangeritin, carotene.

Pharmacological action: Naringin, similar to other flavonoids, had anti-inflammation action. Naringin showed protective effect on ectromelia-infected mice anti-irradiation action by prolonging their survival time. It also had anti-spasm action. The fresh fruit juice was reported to have hypoglycemic action as it contained insulin-like substance.

Attributes: It is pungent and bitter in taste and warm in property. Acts on lung and spleen meridians.

Action: To dispel cold, eliminate damp and phlegm, and to arrest emesis or nausea.

Indications: Cough, itching of the throat and profuse expectoration in colds; nausea, vomiting and epigastric distension caused by improper diet or excessive drinking.

Dosage: 3-9 g.

Storage: Preserve in a cool and dry place, protected from moth.

5.9 Flos Carthami (红花， Honghua)

Safflower

Safflower is the dried flower of *Carthamus tinctorius* L. (Fam. Compostiae). It is collected in summer when its color turns from yellow to red, and dried in the shade or in the sun.

Chemical constituents:

1. Organic acids: palmitic acid; myristic acid; lauric acid; stearic acid; arachidic acid; oleic acid; linoleic acid; linolenic acid.

2. Carthamone; neocarthamin carthamin; safflor-yellow A; $15\alpha, 20\beta$-dihydroxy-Δ^4-pregnen-3-one, β-sitosterol.

Pharmacological action: Its decoction can increase coronary flow and lower blood pressure in dogs. A small dose of the decoction mildly stimulates and a large dose inhibits the heart of toads. It also had anti-inflammatory, analgesic sedative and anti-convulsion action.

Attributes: It is pungent in taste and warm in property. Acts on heart and liver meridians.

Action: To activate blood circulation and stimulate menstrual discharge, and to remove blood stasis and relieve pain.

Indications: Amenorrhea, dysmenorrhea; retention of lochia; formation of mass in the abdomen; traumatic injuries or sores with swelling and pain.

Dosage: 3-9 g.

Storage: Preserve in a cool and dry place, protected from moisture and moth.

5.10   Flos Caryophylli (丁香， Dingxiang)

Clove

Clove is the dried flower bud of *Eugenia caryophylata* Thunb. (Fam. Myrtaceae). It is collected when it turns from green to brick-red, and dried in the sun.

Chemical constituents: Eugenol; eugenol acetate; β-caryophyllene; methyl amyl ketone; methyl *n*-heptyl ketone; vanillin; α-humulene; chavicol; α-ylangene; eugenone; eugenin; eugenitin; isoeogenitin; isoeugenitol; kaempferol; rhamnetin; oleanolic acid and eugeniin.

Pharmacological action: Its extract or decoction showed inhibitory action against many pathogens. It also exhibited inhibitory action against flu virus PR8 (in vitro test). The aqueous or ethanol extract or the oil showed paralysis action or lethal action against swine or dog ascariasis in vitro. It was also a fragrant stomachic tonic by relieving abdominal flatulence, strengthening digestive ability and lessening nausea and vomiting. The oil is also a dental analgesic. Eugenol had paralysis, hypotension, respiration inhibition and anti-convulsion effect by intravenous injection in rabbits.

Attributes: It is pungent in taste and warm in property. Acts on spleen, stomach, lung and kidney meridians.

Action: To warm the spleen and stomach, to regulate the adverse flow of the stomach *qi,* and to restore the kidney *yang.*

Indications: Hiccup, vomiting, anorexia, diarrhea and epigastric and abdominal pain with cold sensation in deficiency-cold syndromes of the spleen and stomach; impotence due to deficiency of the kidney *yang.*

Dosage: 1-3g.

Storage: Preserve in a cool and dry place.

5.11 Flos Chrysanthemi (菊花， Juhua)

Chrysanthemun Flower
Chrysanthemun flower is the dried capitulum of *Chrysanthemum morifolium* Ramat. (Fam. Compositae). It is collected in batches in September to November at flowering, dried in the shade or by baking or dried in the sun after fuming and steaming.

Chemical constituents: Chlorochrymorin; 1, 4-epoxy-10(14)-germa-cradiene-3, 5-diol

Pharmacological Action: Its decoction showed the action of dilating arteria coronaria and increasing coronary flow. It also had inhibitory action against Staphylococcus aureus and Shigella dysenteriae, etc. Also showed inhibition against nine skin fungi, against flu virus and leptospirae.

Attributes: It is sweet and bitter in taste and slight cold in property. Acts on lung and liver meridians.

Action: To dispel wind-heat, To subdue hyperactivity of the liver, and improve eyesight.

Indications: Wind-heat type common cold, headache and dizziness; inflammation of the eye; blurred vision.

Dosage: 4.5-9g.

Storage: Preserve in well-sealed containers, stored in a cool and dry place, protected from mould and moth.

5.12 Folium Mori (桑叶， Sangye)

Mulberry Leaf
Mulberry leaf is the dried leaf of *Morus alba* L. (Fam. Moraceae). It is collected at the early frost season, foreign matter removed, and dried in the sun.

Chemical constituents: Rutin, quercetin, isoquercetin, moracetin, astragalin, β-sitosterol, daucosterol, campesterol, Vitamin B_1, B_2, C.

Pharmacological action: The fresh leaf decoction showed antibacterial and leptospiricidal actions and hypoglycemic action in vitro.

Attributes: It is sweet and bitter in taste and cold in property. Acts on lung and liver meridians.

Action: To dispel wind-heat and to remove heat from the lung, to subdue hyperactivity of the liver, and improve eyesight.

Indications: Upper respiratory infection, heat in the lung with dry cough; dizziness, headache, inflammation of the eye, blurred vision.

Dosage: 4.5-9g.
Storage: Preserve in a dry place.

5.13 Folium Nelumbinis (荷叶，Heye)

Lotus Leaf
Lotus leaf is the dried leaf of *Nelumbo nucifera* Gaertn (Fam. Nymphaeaceae). It is collected in summer and autumn, dried in the sun to remove most of water, removed from the petioles, folded to semi-rounded or plicate, and dried again.

Chemical constituents:
1. Alkanoids: roemerine; nuciferine; lostusine; liensinine; oxyoshinunine; N-norarmepavine; dehydroroemerine; dehydronuciferine; dehydroannoanaine; N-methyl-isocolauine; N-norniferine; nornuciferine; armepavine; pronuciferine, anonaine; D-N-methyleoclaurine.

2. Flavonoids: quercetin; isoquercetin; nelumboside.

3. Organic acids: tartaric acid; citric acid; malic acid; gluconic acid; oxalic acid; succinic acid; palmitic acid.

Pharmacological action: The leaf extract and decoction showed direct vasodilatation action and moderate hypotensive effect on experimental animals. An active component nuciferine exerts antispasmodic effect on smooth muscles.

Attributes: It is bitter in taste and mild in property. Acts on liver, spleen and stomach meridians.

Action: To relieve summer-heat, to invigorate the spleen function and arrest bleeding by reducing heat in blood.

Indications: Summer-heat with dire thirst; diarrhea caused by summer-damp or hypofunction of the spleen; spitting of blood, epistaxis, hematochezia and abnormal uterine bleeding caused by heat in blood.

Dosage: 3-9g.
Storage: Preserve in a ventilated dry place, protected from moth.

5.14 Folium Perillae (紫苏叶，Zisuye)

Perilla Leaf
Perilla leaf is the dried leaf of *Perilla frutescens* (L.) Britt. (Fam. Labiatae). It is collected in summer when the foliage is growing luxuriantly, foreign matter is removed and it is dried in the sun.

Chemical constituents: Perilladehyde; L-limonene; α-pinene; isoegomaketone; isoarnyl 3-furyl ketone; β-pinene; L-linalool; camphene;

menthol; menthone; perilla alcohol; dihydroperilla alcohol; eugenol; perilla ketone; β-dehydroelscholtzione; elemicin; perillanin; cyanidin-3-(6-ρ-coumaroyl-β-D-glucosyl)-5-β-D-glucoside.

Pharmacological action: The leaf decoction or extract 2g/kg PO to rabbits with typhoid fever showed weak antipyretic effect. In vitro studies the leaf inhibited the growth of staphylococcus. The main active constituent, perillaldehyde, showed stronger hyperglycemic action than its oil when made into Oxim.

Attributes: It is pungent in taste and warm in property. Acts on lung and spleen meridians.

Action: To induce perspiration and dispel cold, and to regulate the stomach function.

Indications: Common cold with cough and nausea; vomiting of pregnancy; fish or crab poisoning.

Dosage: 4.5-9g.

Storage: Preserve in a cool and dry place.

5.15 Fructus Amomi (砂仁， Sharen)

Villous Amomum Fruit

Villous Amomum fruit is the dried ripe fruit of *Amomum villosum* Lour. *Amomum villosum* Lour. *Var. Xanthioides* T. L. Wu *et* Senjen or *Amomum longiligulare* T. L. Wu (Fam. Zingiberaceae). It is collected between summer and autumn when ripe, and dried in the sun or at a low temperature.

Chemical constituents: D-campor, d-borneol, bornylacetate, linalool, nerolidol, limonene.

Pharmacological action: The volatile oil and aqueous decoction was inhibitory against Staphylococcus aureus. It had anti-ulcer effect. The aqueous decoction 0.25-0.75 percent excited the isolated intestines, while 1-1.25 percent decoction showed inhibitory action.

Attributes: It is pungent in taste and warm in property. Acts on spleen, stomach and kidney meridians.

Action: To eliminate damp and improve appetite, to warm the spleen and check diarrhea, and to prevent abortion.

Indications: Accumulation of damp in the spleen and the stomach marked by epigastric stuffiness and anorexia; vomiting and diarrhea in deficiency-cold syndrome of the spleen and the stomach; pernicious vomiting of pregnancy; threatened abortion.

Dosage: 3-6g.
Storage: Preserve in a cool and dry place.

5.16 Fructus Anisi Stellati (八角茴香，Bajiaohuixiang)

Chinese Star Anise

Chinese star anise is the dried ripe fruit of *Illcium verum* Hook. f. (Fam. Magnoliaceae). It is collected in autumn and winter when it turns yellow from green, and dried after a brief treatment in boiling water or dried directly.

Chemical constituents: The constituents of *Illcium varum* include volatile oils of *trans*-anethole, *cis*-anethole, α-pinene, camphene, β-pinene, myrcene, α-phellandrene, α-limonene, Δ^3-carene, cineole, thujene, α-terpinene, linalool, terpinene-4-ol, estragole, anisadehyde, α-bergamotene, Z-β-farnesene, *trans*-caryophyllene, terephthaldehyde, β-bisabolene, α-humullene, methyl-3-methoxybenzoate, β-selinene, α-copaene, ρ-methoxy-phenyl-propanone, δ-cadinene, β-guaiene, γ-cadinene, nerolidol, elemol, methylisoeugenol, β-maaliene, carotyol, cedrol, feniculine, methyl chavicol, anisic acid, anisyl acetate, safrole,

Pharmacological action: Its alcoholic extracts showed inhibitory action against Staphylococcus aureu in vitro.

Attributes: It is pungent in taste and warm in property. Acts on liver, spleen, kidney and stomach meridians.

Action: To dispel cold to regulate the flow of *qi* and to relieve pain.

Indications: Abdominal colic; lumbago due to deficiency in the kidney; vomiting and eqigastric pain due to cold in the stomach.

Dosage: 3-6g.
Storage: Preserve in a cool and dry place.

5.17 Fructus Aurantii (代代花，Daidaihua)

Orange Fruit

Orange fruit is the dried, immature fruit of *Citrus aurantium* L. '*Daidai*'. (Fam. Rutaceae). It is collected in July when the fruit is still green and cut into two parts, dried in the sun or at a low temperature.

Chemical constituents: hesperidin, neohesperidin, citromotrin, tangeritin.

Pharmacological action: Its decoction inhibits the intestines in mice or in rabbits in vitro, stimulates the intestines in dogs with gastric fistula and intestinal fistula, and also induces contraction of gravid or non-gravid in rabbits both in vivo and in vitro.

Attributes: It is bitter and sour in taste and slight cold in property. Acts on lung, spleen, stomach and large intestine meridians.

Action: To regulate the flow of *qi*, remove its stagnation, and alleviate distension.

Indications: Distension and pain in the chest and hypochondriac regions due to stagnation of *qi*; indigestion with retention of phlegm and fluid; gastroptosis, prolapse of the rectum, prolapse of the uterus.

Dosage: 3-9g.

Storage: Preserve.

5.18 Fructus Canarii (青果， Qingguo)

Chinese White Olive

Chinese white olive is the dried ripe fruit of *Canarium album* Raeusch. (Fam. Bruseraceae). It is collected in autumn when ripe, and dried.

Chemical constituents: Proteins (1.20 percent), cabohydrates (12 percent), Vitamin C (0.02 percent), Ca (0.24 percent), P (0.05 percent), Fe (0.0014 percent), amyrin.

Pharmacological action: Its extracts can protect the liver and increase the secretion of saliva.

Attributes: It is sweet and sour in taste and mild in property. Acts on lung and stomach meridians.

Action: To remove heat and cure sore throat, to promote the production of body fluid, and counteract toxicity.

Indications: Pain and swelling of the throat, cough; dire thirst; fish or crab poisoning.

Dosage: 4.5-9g.

Storage: Preserve in a dry place, protected from moth.

5.19 Fructus Cannabis (火麻仁， Huomaren)

Hemp Seed

Hemp seed is the dried ripe fruit of *Cannabis sativa* L. (Fam. Moraceae). It is collected in autumn when ripe, foreign matter removed and dried in the sun.

Chemical constituents:

1. Organic acids: palmitic acid, oleic acid, stearic acid, methyl palmitate, methyl oleate, methyl stearate.

2. Steroids: 5α-ergostane-3-one, 5α-stigmastane-3-one, campeaterol, stigmasterol, β-sitosterol.

3. Lignanamides: cannabisin A, B, C, D; grossamide; N-*trans*-caffeoyltyramine; N-*trans*-feruoyl-tyramine; N-ρ-coumaroyltyramine.

4. Cannabiols: cannabinol; cannabidiol; Δ^9-tetrehydrocannabinol; cannabingelol.

5. Flavonoids: cannflavin A, B.

6. Others: vitamin B; choline; trigonelline; torigomelline.

Pharmacological action: It stimulated intestinal mucous membrane, fastened peristalsis and decreased the water absorption in large intestines, so caused cathartic effect. It also lowers the blood pressure in anesthetized cats and normal rats.

Attributes: It is sweet in taste and mild in property. Acts on spleen, stomach and large intestine meridians.

Action: To cause laxation.

Indications: Constipation due to deficiency of blood and intestinal fluid.

Dosage: 9-15g.

Storage: Preserve in a cool and dry place, protected from heat and moth.

5.20   Fructus Chaenomelis (木瓜，Mugua)

Common Floweringqince Fruit

Common Floweringqince fruit is the dried nearly ripe fruit of *Chaenomeles speciosa* (Sweet) Nakai (Fam. Rosaceae). It is collected in summer and autumn when it turns greenish-yellow, boiled in water until the exocarp becomes greyish-white in color, halved longitudinally, and dried in the sun.

Chemical constituents: The major constituents of the fruits of *Chaenomeles speciosa* are organic acids such as malic acid, tartaric acid, citric acid, ascorbic acid, fumaric acid and oleanolic acid.

Pharmacological action: The decoction showed marked inhibitory action against immunomechanic arthritis in mice. Its solution had inhibitory action against Ehrlich ascitic carcinoma in mice.

Attributes: It is sour in taste and warm in property. Acts on liver and spleen meridians.

Action: To lessen contracture, regulate stomach function, and dispel damp.

Indications: Arthritis with ankylosis, aching and heaviness senation of the loins and knees; systremma due to vomiting and diarrhea; edema and weakness of the legs.

Dosage: 6-9g.

Storage: Preserve in a dry place, protected from moisture and moth.

5.21 Fructus Citri (香缘，Xiangyuan)

Citron Fruit

Citron fruit is the dried ripe fruit of *Citrus medica* L. or *Citrus wilsonii* Tanaka (Fam. Rutaceae). It is collected in autumn when ripe, cut fresh, dried in the sun or at a low temperature.

Chemical constituents:

1. Volatile oils: dipetene, α-limonene, citral, phellandrene, gerany acetate, linalyl acetate, geraniol, geranial, neral, nerol.

2. Diterpenoids: citropten, limonin, obacunone, normilin.

3. Organic acids: citric acid, malic acid, succinic acid, valencic acid.

4. Others: citflavanone, hesperidin, vitamin C, choline, etrogol.

Pharmacological action: Accelerating gastrointestinal peristalsis and eliminating phlegm.

Attributes: It is pungent, bitter and sour in taste and warm in property. Acts on liver, spleen and lung meridians.

Action: To regulate the flow of *qi* in the liver, spleen and stomach, and to resolve phlegm.

Indications: Stagnation of *qi* in the liver and stomach manifested by distending pain in the chest and hypochondria, fullness and stuffiness sensation in the epigastrium, vomiting and belching; cough with copious expectoration.

Dosage: 3-9g.

Storage: Preserve in a cool and dry place, protected from mould and moth.

5.22 Fructus Citri Sarcodactylis (佛手，Foshou)

Finger Citron

Finger citron is the dried fruit of *Citrus medica* L. *var. sarcodactylis* Swingle (Fam. Rutaceae). It is collected in autumn when the fruit is turning yellow or not, cut lingitudinally into slices, dried in the sun or at a low temperature.

Chemical constituents:

1. Coumarins: citropten; 6,7-dimethoxycoumarin; cis-head-to-tail-lemittin dimer; cis-head-to-head-lemittin dimer.

2. Organic acids: p-hydroxyphenylpropenoic acid; succicic acid; palmitic acid.

3. Flavonoids: 3,5,8-trihydroxy-3`, 4`-dimethoxyflavone; diosmin; hesperidin, citflavanone; 3, 5, 6-trihydroxy-4`, 7`-dimethoxyflavone; 3, 5, 6-trihydroxy-3`, 4`, 7`-trimethoxyflavone.

4. Diterpenoids: normilin; limenin.

Pharmacological action: The ethanol extract relaxes the spasm of smooth muscles of the gastrointestine, gallbladder and bronchus. Intravenous injection in cats also inhibited heart and showed hypotensive effect. Its volatile oil is an expectorant and antiasthmatic.

Attributes: It is pungent, bitter and sour in taste and warm in property. Acts on liver, spleen and lung meridians.

Action: To regulate the *qi* of the liver and stomach, and to relieve pain.

Indications: Stagnation of *qi* in the liver and stomach marked by distension and pain in the chest and hypochondria regions, stuffiness feeling in the stomach, anorexia and vomiting.

Dosage: 3-9g.

Storage: Preserve in a cool and dry place, protected from mould and moth.

5.23 Fructus Crataegi (山楂， Shanzha)

Hawthorn Fruit

Hawthorn fruit is the dried ripe fruit of *Crataegus pinnatifida* Bge. *var. major* N. E. Br., or *Crataegus pinnatifida* Bge. (Fam. Rosaceae). It is collected in autumn when ripe,cut into slices, and dried.

Chemical constituents:

1. Flavonoids: hyperoside; quercetin; vitexin; rutin; epicatechin; eriodictyol-3, 7-diglucopyranoside and flavan polymers.

2. Organic acids: Citric acid; chorogenic acid; ursolic acid; oxalic acid; malic acid; oleanolic acid; palmitic acid; stearic acid; oleic acid; linoleic acid; linolenic acid; succinic acid.

3. Others: methy-hexane; heptane; methylcyclohexane; 2-methyl-heptane; methyl-benzene; 1,3-dimethyl-cis-cyclohexane; 1,2,3-trimethyl-cyclopetane; 2,3,4-trmethyl-hexane; 1,4-dimethyl-cis-cyclohexane; 2-methyl-octane; ethyl-cyclohexane; 1, 3, 5-trimethyl-cyclohexane; 2,3-dimethylheptane; 3,5-dimethyl-butyl-benzene; 1,2,3-trimethyl-

cyclohexane; 1,2-dimethyl-benzene; 3-ethyl-2, 3-dimethylpetane; 3, 4, 4-trimethyl-2-hexane; 1-propenyl-cyclohexane; propyl-cyclohexane; 3-methy-1,2-cyclopentanediol; 4-methyl-nonane; 2, 4-dimethyl-undecane; (1S, 3S)-(+)-m-mentane; 1-ethyl-2-methylbenzene; decane; 1, 2, 3-trimethyl-benzene; 5-ethyl-2-methyl-hepatane; butyl-cyclohexane.

Pharmacological action: The fluid extract, flavones, hydrolysis product, and triterpenic acid from the fruit had cardiotonic effect and produced slow but prolonged hypotensive action in anesthetized animals and definite inhibitory action on arrhythmia of experimental animals. The extract lowered serum cholesterol and triglyceride levels in rabbits, showing its anti-hyper lipidemia effect. The fruit decoction or the 95 percent alcohol extract of either the crude or charred fruit showed definite antibacterial actions.

Attributes: It is sour and sweet in taste and slightly warm in property. Acts on spleen, stomach and liver meridians.

Action: To stimulate digestion and promote the functional activity of the stomach; to improve the normal flow of *qi* and dissipate blood stasis.

Indications: Stagnation of undigested meat with epigastric distension, diarrhea and abdominal pain; amenorrhea due to blood stasis, eplgastric pain or abdominal colic, after childbirth; heraial pain; hyperlipemia.

Dosage: 9-12g.

Storage: Preserve in a ventilated dry place, protected from moth.

5.24 Fructus Foeniculi (小茴香， Xiaohuixiang)

Fennel

Fennel is the dried ripe fruit of *Foeniculum vulgare* Mill. (Fam. Umbelliferae). The plant is cut in autumn when the fruit is nearly ripe and dried in the sun and then it is tapped off and foreign matter removed.

Chemical constituents:

1. Volatile oils: anethole; anisaldehyde; fenchone; α-pinene; α-phellandrene; camphene; dipentane; anisic acid; estragole; *cis*-anethole; ρ-cymene; ligustilide; butylidenephthalide.

2. Amino acids: glutamic acid; glutamine; aspargic acid; asparagine; proline; arginine; alanine; γ-aminobutyric acid.

3. Steroids: phytosteryl-β-fructofuranoside; β-sitosterol; stigmasterol; Δ^7-stigmasterol; campesterol.

4. Others: petroselic acid; oleanolic acid; 7-hydroxycoumarin; 6, 7-dihydroxycoumarin; palmatic acid; choline; acetylcholine; behenic acid.

Pharmacological action: Its oil can increase the effect of streptomycin on experimental tuberculosis in mice. Its decoction can accelerate gastrointestinal peristalsis and promote eliminating of flatus. It also has the action of eliminating phlegm.

Attributes: It is pungent in taste and warm in property. Acts on liver, kidney, spleen and stomach meridians.

Action: To dispel cold and relieve pain, to regulate the stomach function.

Indications: Scrotal hernia with pain and cold extremities; dysmenorrhea with lower abdominal pain and cold extremities; dysmenorrhea with lower abdominal pain and cold sensation; distending pain in the epigastrium with anorexia, vomiting and diarrhea; hydrocele of tunica vaginalis.

Dosage: 3-6g.

Storage: Preserve in a cool and dry place.

5.25 Fructus Gardeniae (栀子， Zhizi)

Cape Jasmine Fruit

Cape Jasmine fruit is the dried ripe fruit of *Gardenia jasminoides* Ellis (Fam. Rubiaceae). It is collected from September to November when it turns reddish-yellow, removed from the fruit stalk and foreign matter, steamed thoroughly or treated with boiling water for a moment, then dried.

Chemical constituents:

1. Glycosides: gardenoside; geniposide; genipingentiobioside; shanzhiside; gardoside; scandoside methyl ester; deacetylasperulosidic acid methyl ester; geniposidic acid; 10-O-acetylgeniposide; 6``-O-ρ-acoumaroyl-genipin-gentiobioside; 1-β-glucogeniposide.

2. Organic acids: chlorogenic acid; 3, 4-di-O-caffeoylquinic acid; 3-O-caffeoyl-4-O-sinapoyl-quinic acid; 3, 5-di-O-caffeoyl-4-O- (3-hydroxy-3-methyl)-glutaroylquinic acid; 3, 4-dicaffeoyl-5- (3-hydroxy-5-methylglutaroyl)-quinic acid; jasminoidin; picrocrocinic acid.

3. Others: gardenin; crocin; crocetin; α-crocetin; D-mannitol; β-sitosterol; nonacosane; ursolic acid.

Pharmacological action: Its extract attenuated carbon tetrachloride-induced liver damage. Experiments on rats and rabbits indicated that it had cholagogic and choleric actions. Its ethanol extract decreased the spontaneous activity of the animals indicating its sedative effect and it also had antipyretic action. Its decoction or ethanol extract showed hypotensive effect in experimental animals. It showed anti-bacterial effect and in vitro inhibitory actions against various skin fungi.

Attributes: It is bitter in taste and cold in property. Acts on heart, lung and *sanjiao* meridians.

Action: To reduce fire and ease the mind, to eliminate damp-heat, and to remove heat from blood and counteract toxicity.

Indications: Febrile diseases with restlessness; jaundice with dark urine; hematuria with difficult painful urination; hemoptysis and epistaxis caused by heat in the blood; inflammation of the eye; boils and sores; external use for sprains and bruises.

Dosage: 6-9g.

Storage: Preserve in a ventilated dry place.

5.26 Fructus Hippophae (沙棘，Shaji)

Seabuckthorn Fruit

Seabuckthorn fruit is the dried ripe fruit of *Hippophae rhamnoides* L. (Fam. Flaeagnaceae). It is collected in autumn and winter when ripe or frozen hard, foreign matter removed, and dried or dried after steaming.

Chemical constituents:

1. Vitamins: Vitamin C, A, E, B_1, B_2, B_{12}, K and folic acid.

2. Flavonoids: quercetin; isorhamnetin; astragalin; rutin; amyrin; kampferol; myricetin.

3. Organic acid: gallic acid; catechinic acid; ursolic acid; oleanolic acid; chlorogenic acid; acetic acid; butyric acid; caproic acid; caprylic acid; capric acid; lauric acid; myristic acid; palmitoleic acid; linoleic acid; linolenic acid; stearic acid; malic acid; citric acid; tartaric acid; oxalic acid; succinic acid; arachidic acid; *cis*-vaccenic (11-octadecenoic) acid; 11-hydroxy-9-tricenoic acid; 9-hydroxy-10, 12-pentadecadienoic acid; 13-hydroxy-9, 11-hexadecadienoic acid; 9, 12-dihydroxy-15-nonadecenoic acid.

4. Saccharides: glucose, fructose.

Pharmacological action: Its seed oil can protect the liver from damage and promote the repair of gastric ulcers.

Attributes: It is sour in taste and warm in property. Acts on liver and kidney meridians.

Action: To relieve cough and promote expectoration, to promote digestion and remove stagnancy of food, and to promote blood circulation and remove blood stasis.

Indications: Cough with profuse expectoration; indigestion, stagnancy of food with abdominal pain; traumatic swelling and ecchymoses; amenorrhea due to blood stasis.

Dosage: 3-9g.

Storage: Preserve in a cool and dry place, protected from mould and moth.

5.27 Fructus Hordei Germinatus (麦芽，Maiya)

Germinated Barley

Germinated barley is the dried germinated ripe fruit of *Hordeum vulgare* L. (Fam. Gramineae). It is soaked in water at an appropriate temperature and moisture until the budlet grows up to about 5 mm long, and dried.

Chemical constituents: Vitamin D, E; phospholipid; dextrin; maltose; hordenine; hordatine A; hordanine B; cytochrome C; α-tocotrienol; α-tocopheryl quinone; saponarin and lutonarin.

Pharmacological action: Its decoction promotes the secretion of pepsin and gastric juice.

Attributes: It is sweet in taste and mild in property. Acts on spleen and stomach meridians.

Action: To invigorate the function of the spleen, to regulate the function of the stomach, and to promote the flow of milk.

Indications: Anorexia due to diminished function of the spleen; galactostasis.

Dosage: 9-15g.

Storage: Preserve in a ventilated dry place, protected from moth.

5.28 Fructus Jujubae (大枣，Dazao)

Chinese Date

Chinese date is the dried ripe fruit of *Ziziphus jujuba* Mill (Fam. Rhamnaceae). It is collected in autumn when ripe, and dried in the sun.

Chemical constituents:

1. Organic acids: betulinic acid; oleanolic acid; maslinic acid; malic acid; tartaric acid; catechin; oleic acid; linoleic acid; palmitic acid; stearic acid; myristic acid.

2. Triterpenoids: 3-O-*trans*-ρ-coumaroyl maslinic acid; 3-O-*cis*-ρ-

coumaroyl maslinic acid; 3-O-*trans*-ρ-coumaroyl alphitolic acid; 2-O-*trans*-ρ-coumaroyl alphitolic acid; 3-O-*cis*-ρ-coumaroyl alphitolic acid; zizyphus saponin I, II, II, jujuboside A, B; zizybeoside I, II; zizyvoside I, II and roseoside.

3. Alkaloids: stepharine; N-nornuciferine; asimilobine; daechualkaloic A.

4. Flavonoids: 6, 8-di-C-glucopyranosyl-2 (*S*)-naringenin; 6, 8-di-C-glucopyranosyl-2(*R*)-naringenin; swertisin; spinosin; 6```-sinapoylspinosin; 6```-feruloylspinosin; 6```-ρ-coumaroylspinosin; rutin.

5. Saccharides: Glucose; fructose; zizyphus-pectin.

6. Vitamin: Vitamin C; riboflacine; thiamine; carotine; nicotic acid.

Pharmacological action: The ethanol extract showed sedative, mesmerism and hypotensive action, and the decoction showed the action of protecting the liver, anticancer, antimutation and enhancing muscle strength.

Attributes: It is sweet in taste and warm in property. Acts on spleen and stomach meridians.

Action: To tonify the spleen and replenish *qi*, to nourish blood, and to ease the mind

Indications: Anorexia, lassitude and loose stools in deficiency syndromes of the spleen; hysteria in women.

Dosage: 6-15g.

Storage: Preserve in a dry place, protected from moth.

5.29 Fructus Lycii (枸杞子， Gouqizi)

Barbary Wolfberry Fruit

Barbary wolfberry fruit is the dried ripe fruit of *Lycium barbarum* L. (Fam. Solanaceae). It is collected in summer and autumn when the fruit turns orange-red.

Chemical constituents: Carotene, thamine, riboflavine, nicotinic acid, ascorbic acid, β-sitosterol, linoleic acid, zeaxanthin, betanine, physalien, cryptoxanthin, astropine, hyoscuyamine, acopoletin.

Pharmacological action: The aqueous extract enhanced nonspecific immunity in mice. It also can relieve the liver damage induced by CCl_4 in mice.

Attributes: It is sweet in taste and mild in property. Acts on liver and kidney meridians.

Action: To benefit the liver and the kidney, to replenish vital essence and to improve eyesight.

Indications: General debility with deficiency of vital essence manifested by aching of the loins and knees, dizziness and tinnitus; diabetes caused by internal heat; anemia; impaired vision.

Dosage: 6-12g.

Storage: Preserve in a cool and dry place, protected from mould and moth.

5.30 Fructus Momordicae (罗汉果， Luohanguo)

Grosvenor Momordica Fruit

Grosvenor Momordica fruit is the dried fruit of *Momordica grosvenori* Swingle (Fam. Cucurbitaceae). It is collected in autumn when it turns from pale green to deep green, and dried in the air for several days at a low temperature.

Chemical constituents:

1. Triterpenoids: mogrol, mogroside II_E, III, III_E, IV, V, 11-oxomogroside V, mogroester, neomogroside.

2. Flavonoids: grosvenorine, kaempferol-3, 7-di-O-rhamnopyranoside.

3. Organic acids: linoleic acid, oleic acid, palmitic acid, stearic acid.

4. Others: vitamin C.

Pharmacological action: Its decoction showed the actions of an expectorant, antitussive and antiasthmatic.

Attributes: It is sweet in taste and cool in property. Acts on lung and large intestine meridians.

Action: To remove heat, moisten the lung and relax the bowels.

Indications: Dry cough, sore throat and hoarseness of voice due to heat in the lung; constipation.

Dosage: 9-15g.

Storage: Preserve in a dry place, protected from mould and moth.

5.31 Fructus Mori (桑椹， Sangshen)

Mulberry Fruit

Mulberry fruit is the dried fruit-spike of *Morus alba* L. (Fam. Moraceae). It is collected in April-June when the fruit turns red, dried in the sun, or dried after steaming briefly.

Chemical constituents: Vitamin B_1, B_2, C; saccharides and proteins.

Pharmacological action: Its decoction moderately induced lymphocyte transformation.

Attributes: It is sweet and sour in taste and cold in property. Acts on heart, liver and kidney meridians.

Action: To nourish yin and blood and promote the production of body fluid.

Indications: Vertigo and tinnitus, palpitation, insomnia, premature greying of hair and beard; thirst due to impairment of body fluid; diabetes caused by internal heat; constipation due to deficiency of blood.

Dosage: 9-15g.

Storage: Preserve in a ventilated dry place, protected from moth.

5.32 Fructus Mume (乌梅, Wumei)

Smoked Plum

Smoked plum is the dried almost ripe fruit of *Prunus mume* (Sieb.) Sieb. Et Zucc. (Fam. Rosaceae). It is collected in summer when almost ripe, baked at a low temperature, and covered until turns black in color.

Chemical constituents:

1. Volatile oils: n-hexanal; trans-2-hexanal; n-hexanol; trans-2-hexen-1-ol; cis-3-hexen-1-ol; linalool; α-terpineol; geraiol; trimethyltetra-hydrophthalene derivates; tetradecanoic acid; benzaldehyde; terpinen-4-ol; bezylazlcohol; hexadecanoic acid.

2. Lipids: neutral lipids, glycolipis, phospholipids, free sterols, sterol esters.

3. Organic acids: citric acid, succinic acid, fumaric acid.

4. Triterpenoids: lup-20- (29)-ene, 7β, 15α-diol-3β-palmitate, stearate, arachidate, behenate and lignocerate.

5. Flavonoids: Rhamncitrin-3-O-rhamnopyranoside; kaempferol-3-O-rhamnopyranoside; rhamnetin-3-O-rhamnopyranoside and quercetin-3-O-rhamnopyranoside.

6. Others: amygdalin.

Pharmacological action: Its decoction showed antibacterial effect. The aqueous decoction in vitro had antifungal action.

Attributes: It is sour in taste and mild in property. Acts on liver, spleen, lung and large intestine meridians.

Action: To arrest persistent cough, relieve diarrhea by astringing the intestines, promote the production of body fluid, and relieve colic caused by ascaris.

Indications: Persistent cough in deficiency syndromes of the lung; chronic dysentery and diarrhea; thirst in consumptive diseases; colic and vomiting caused by ascaris, biliary ascariasis.

Dosage: 6-12g.

Storage: Preserve in a cool and dry place, protected from moisture.

5.33 Fructus Piperis (胡椒，Hujiao)

Pepper Fruit

Pepper fruit is the dried nearly ripe or ripe fruit of *Piper nigrum* L. (Fam. Piperaceae). It is collected in late autumn to next spring when the fruit is in dark green, dried in the sun, and it is known as "black pepper." If it is collected when it turns to red, and moistened for several days, removed from sarcocarp, and dried in the sun, it is known as "white pepper".

Chemical constituents:

1. Volatile oils: piperonal, dihydrocarveol, β-caryophyllene, caryophyllene oxide, α-pinene, β-pinene, sabinene, myrcene, limonene, ρ-cymene, cryptone, *cis*-ρ-2-menten-1-ol, *cis*-ρ-2,8-menthadieon-1-ol, *trans*-pinocarveol, safrole.

2. Alkaloids: piperine, piperanine, chavicine, pipercide, piperamide I, II, III, IV, V; ([2*E*, 4*E*]-2, 4-decadienoyl)-pyrrolidine; 1-([2*E*, 4*E*]-2, 4-dodecadienoyl)-pyrrolidine.

3. Others: 3, 4-dihydroxyphenylethanol glycoside; O-diphenol oxide.

Pharmacological action: It can increase secretion of digestive system and promote gastrointestinal peristalsis by oral administration. The piperine is an antipyretic and wind-expelling agent.

Attributes: It is pungent in taste and hot in property. Acts on stomach and large intestine meridians.

Action: To dispel cold from the stomach, and to eliminate phlegm.

Indications: Vomiting, abdominal pain diarrhea and anorexia due to cold in the stomach; epilepsy with much phlegm.

Dosage: 0.6-1.5g.

Storage: Preserve in well closed containers, stored in a cool and dry place.

5.34 Herba Cichorii (菊苣，Juju)

Chicory Herb

Chicory herb is the aerial part of *Cichorium glandulosum* Boiss. Et Hout and *Cichorium intybus* L. (Fam.Compositae). It is collected in autumn, foreign matter removed, and dried in the sun.

Chemical constituents: esculetin, esculin, cichorin, lactucin, lactucopicrin, α-lactucerol, monocaffeyltataric acid and chicoric acid.

Pharmacological action: Its decoction showed the action of antibacteric.

Attributes: It is slightly bitter and salty in taste and cool in property. Acts on stomach and liver meridians.

Action: To remove heat from the liver, stimulate the discharge of bile, promote digestion and increase appetite, and cause diuresis.

Indications: Jaundice caused by damp-heat; epigastric pain with impairment of appetite; edema with oliguria.

Dosage: 9-18g.

Storage: Preserve in a cool and dry place.

5.35 Herba Moslae (香薷, Xiangru)

Haichow Elsholtzia Herb

Haichow Elsholtzia herb is the dried aerial part of *Mosla chinensis* Maxim. It is collected in summer and autumn when the foliage is growing luxuriantly and the fruit ripening. Foreign matter is removed and it is dried in the sun.

Chemical constituents: carvacrol; α-*trans*-bergamotene; β-caryophyllene; thymol; humulene; β-bisabolene; terpinen-4-ol; γ-terpinene; p-cymene; α-phemmandrene; β-pinene; camphene and α-pinene.

Pharmacological action: Its volatile oil causes dilation and congestion of renal blood vessels and exerts a diuretic effect. It also can act as an expectorant.

Attributes: It is pungent in taste and slightly warm in property. Acts on lung and stomach meridians.

Action: To induce diaphoresis, regulate the function of the spleen and the stomach, and remove damp through diuresis.

Indications: Attack of summer heat and damp manifested by chills and fever, headache, abdominal pain, vomiting, diarrhea, oliguria and no sweating.

Dosage: 3-9g.

Storage: Preserve in a cool and dry place.

5.36 Herba Menthae (薄荷，Bohe)

Peppermint

Peppermint is the dried aerial part of *Mentha haplocalyx* Briq. (Fam. Labiatae). It is collected in summer and autumn when foliage grows luxuriantly or in the third round of flowering. It is gathered in several times on fine days, and dried in the sun or in the shade.

Chemical constituents: Menthol, menthone, menthyl acetate, camphene, limonene, isomenthone, pinene, menthenone, isoraifolin, luteolin-7-O-glucopyranoside, menthoside, rosmarinic acid.

Pharmacological action: Menthol and menthone possess analgesic, cancer-preventive and sedative activities.

Attributes: It is pungent in taste and cool in property. Acts on lung and liver meridians.

Action: To dispel wind-heat from the head and eyes, and to promote eruption.

Indications: Headache in influenza, upper respiratory infection and other epidemic febrile diseases at the initial stage; inflammation of the eye, sore throat, ulcers in the mouth; rubella measles; discomfort with feeling of distension in the chest and hypochondriac regions.

Dosage: 3-6g.

Storage: Preserve in a cool and dry place.

5.37 Herba Pogostemonis (广藿香，Guanghuoxiang)

Cablin Patchouli Herb

Cablin Patchouli herb is the dried aerial part of *Pogostemon cablin* (Blanco) Benth. (Fam.Labiatae). It is collected when foliage grows luxuriantly, exposed to the sun by day and closed tightly at night repeatedly until completely dried.

Chemical constituents:

1. Volatile oils: methylchavicol, anethole, anisaldehyde, d-limonene, p-methoxycinnamaldehyde, α-pinene, β-pinene, 3-octanone, 3-octanol, ρ-cymene, 1-octen-3-ol, linalool, 1-caryophyllene, β-elemene, β-humulene, α-ylangene, β-farnesene, γ-cadinene, calamenene, *cis*-β-hexenal, *cis*-γ-hexenal.

2. Flavonoids: acacetin; 5,7-dihysroxy-4`-methoxyflavone; tilianine; 5-hydroxy-4`-methoxy-7-glucopyranosylflavone; linarin; acacetin-7-O-rutinoside; agastachoside; 7-O-(6``-O-acetyl)-β-D-glucopyranosyl-5-

hydroxy-4`-methoxyflavone; isoagastachoside; 2``-O-acetyltilianine; agastachin.

Pharmacological action: The decoction of the herb showed antifungal, spirocheticidal and antiviral activities. In addition, acacetin possesses antiallergic activity.

Attributes: It is pungent in taste and sight warm in property. Acts on spleen, stomach and lung meridians.

Action: To resolve turbid damp, improve appetite, arrest vomiting and dispel summer-heat or summer-damp.

Indications: Lingering of turbid damp in the spleen and stomach manifested by stuffiness in the epigastrium and vomiting; summer-damp affection marked by lassitude and stuffiness in the chest; cold-damp affection in summer time marked by abdominal pain, vomiting and diarrhea; sinusitis with headache.

Dosage: 3-9g.

Storage: Preserve in a cool and dry place, protected from moisture.

5.38 Herba Portulacae (马齿苋，Machixian)

Purslane Herb

Purslane herb is the dried aerial part of *Portulaca oleracea* L. (Fam. Portulacaceae). It is collected in summer and autumn, the remains of roots and foreign matter removed, it is washed clean, steamed briefly or treated with boiling water, and then dried in the sun.

Chemical constituents:

1. Triterpenoids: β-amyrin, butyrospermol, parkeol, cycloartenol, 24-methylene-24-dihydroparkeol, 24-methylene cycloartanol.

2. Flavonoids: quercetin, kaempferol, myricetin, apigenin, luteolin.

3. Amono acids: glutamic acid, glutamine, aspartic acid, asparagine, propline, arginine, alanine, γ-aminobutyric acid, dopamine, dopa.

4. Malic acid, α-linolenic aicid, nicotinic acid, thiamine, riboflavine, vitamin A, B_1, lutein, β-carotene, α-tocopherol, β-sitosterol, stigmasterol, campesterol, glucose, fructose.

Pharmacological action: The decoction of the herb possesses antiseptic and blood pressure increasing activity.

Attributes: It is sour in taste and cold in property. Acts on liver and large intestine meridians.

Action: To remove toxic heat, and to arrest bleeding.

Indications: Dysentery with bloody stools; boils and sores, eczema, erysipelas; snake or insect bite; hematochezia, hemorrhoidal bleeding, abnormal uterine bleeding.

Dosage: 9-15g of the dried herb or 30-60g of the fresh herb for oral administration; appropriate quantity of the fresh herb to be pounded into paste for topical application.

Storage: Preserve in a ventilated dry place, protected from moisture.

5.39 Mel (蜂蜜，Fengmi)

Honey

Honey is a saccharine fluid deposited by *Apis cerana* Fabricus or *Apis mellifera* Linnaeus (Fam. Apidae). It is collected from spring to autumn, and filtered.

Chemical constituents: Glucose, fructose, pantothenic acid, nocotinic acid, acetylcholine, Vitamin A, D, E.

Pharmacological action: The food shows laxative, antitumor and detoxicative activity and could increase humoral immune function.

Attributes: It is sweet in taste and mild in property. Acts on lung, spleen and large intestine meridians.

Action: To replenish the spleen and stomach, relieve dryness, alleviate pain, and counteract toxicity.

Indications: Epigastric pain alleviated after meal or by pressing; dry cough; constipation; external use for sores, scalds and burns.

Dosage: 15-30g.

Storage: Preserve in a cool place.

5.40 Pericappium Citri Reticulatae (陈皮，Chenpi)

Dried Tangerine Peel

Dried tangerine peel is the dried pericarp of the ripe fruit of *Citrus reticulata* Balanco or its cultivars (Fam. Rutaceae). It is peeled off when the fruit is ripe and dried in the sun or at a low temperature.

Chemical constituents:

1. Volatile oils: α-thujene, α-pinene, sabinene, β-pinene, β-myrcene, octanal, α-phellandrene, α-terpinene, ρ-cymene, limonene, α-ocimene, γ-terpinene, terpinolene, carene-4, linalool, 3,7-dimenthyl-7-octenal, terpineol-4, α-terpineol, decanal, citronellol, 4-(1, 1-dimethylethyl)-benzenemethanol, perillaldehyde, carvacrol, α-farnesene, benzylalcohol, nerol, octanol, thymol, citronellal, sabinene hydrate, neral, d-limonene.

2. Flavonoids: hesperidin, neohesperidin, tangeretin; 5-hydroxy-6, 7, 8, 3`, 4`-pentamethoxyflavone; 5, 6, 7, 8, 4`-pentamethoxyflavone; 5, 6, 7, 8, 3`, 4`-hexamethoxyflavone.

Pharmacological action: Hesperidin possesses antiallergenic, antioxidative, antistomatitic activity. In mice and in rats, synepherine increased the plasma and myocardial cGMP levels. Continuous iv infusion of 4mg/min synepherine into healthy volunteers significantly increased the systolic and mean arterial blood pressure.

Attributes: It is bitter and pungent in taste and warm in property. Acts on lung and spleen meridians.

Action: To regulate the flow of *qi*, to invigorate the spleen function, to eliminate damp, and to resolve phlegm.

Indications: Distension and fullness sensation in the chest and epigastrium with anorexia, vomiting and diarrhea; cough with copious phlegm.

Dosage: 3 9g.

Storage: Preserve in a cool and dry place, protected from mould and moth.

5.41 Pericarpium Zanthoxyli (花椒， Huajiao)

Pricklyash Peel

Pricklyash peel is the dried pericarp of the ripe fruit of *Zanthoxylum schinifolium* Sieb. Et Zucc. or *Zanthoxylum bungeanum* Maxim. (Fam. Rutaceae). It is collected in autumn when ripe, dried in the sun, seeds and foreign matter are removed.

Chemical constituents:
1. Alkaloids: skimmianine, dictamnine, kokusagine, haplopine.
2. Coumarins: bergapten, herniarin, umbelliferone.
3. Volatile oils: limonene, eucalyptol, myrcene, geraniol, cumic alcohol, chavicol, methyl ether.

Pharmacological action: Skimmianine possesses adrenostimulating, antispasmodic, ecbolic, uterocontractive, hypertensive, hypothermal and myotonic acitivities. Dictamnine also showed cardiotonic and uterocontractive acitivities.

Attributes: It is pungent in taste and warm in property. Acts on spleen, stomach and kidney meridians.

Action: To warm the spleen and the stomach and relieve pain, kill worms, and relieve itching.

108

Indications: Epigastric pain accompanied by cold sensation, vomiting and diarrhea; abdominal pain due to intestinal parasitosis; ascariasis. External use for itching in eczema.

Dosage: 3-6g.

Storage: Preserve in a ventilated dry place.

5.42 Poria (茯苓, Fuling)

Indian Bread

Indian bread is the dried sclerotium of the fungus, *Poria cocos* (Schw.) Wolf (Fam. Polyporaceae). It is collected mostly in July-September, removed from soil, piled up, spread, and air-dried on the surface. Repeat this operation several times until wrinkles appear and the inside water is evaporated, then dry in the shade.

Chemical constituents:

1. Polysaccharides: pochymose (β-pachyman, pachymaran)

2. Triterpenoids: pachymic acid; tumulisic acid; eburicoic acid; piniolic acid; 3β-hydroxylanosta-7, 9(11), 24-trien-21-oic acid; poricoic acid A [16α-hydroxy-3, 4-secolanosta-4(28), 7, 9(11), 24(31)-tetraen-3, 21-dioic acid], poricoic acid B[16α-hydroxy-3, 4-secolanosta-4(28), 7, 9(11), 24-tetraen-3, 21-dioic acid].

3. Fatty acids: caprylic acid; undecanoic acid; lauric acid; dodecenoic acid; palmitic acid.

Pharmacological action: The herb showed diuretic, antitumor, sedative activities. The decoction of the herb showed immune-enhancing activity.

Attributes: It is sweet in taste and mild in property. Acts on heart, lung, spleen and kidney meridians.

Action: To cause diuresis, to invigorate the spleen function, and to calm the mind.

Indications: Edema with oliguria; dizziness and palpitation caused by retained fluid; diminished function of the spleen marked by anorexia, loose stools or diarrhea; restlessness and insomnia.

Dosage: 9-15g.

Storage: Preserve in a dry place, protected from moisture.

5.43 Radix Angelicae Dahuricae (白芷, Baizhi)

Dahurian Angelica Root

Dahurian angelica root is the dried root of *Angelica dahurica* (Fisch. Ex Hoffm.) Benth. Et. Hook. f. or *Angelica dahurica* (Fisch. Ex Hoffm.)

Benth. et Hook. f. *var. formosana* (Boiss.) Shan et Yuan (Fam. Umbelliferae). It is collected in summer and autumn when the leaf turns to yellow, removed from rootlet and soil, and dried in the sun or at a low temperature.

Chemical constituents:

Angelica dahurica

1. Coumarins: byak-angelicin; byak-angelicol; oxypeucedanin; imperatorin; isoimperatorin; phellopterin; xanthotoxin; marmesin; scopoletin; isobyakangelicol; neobyakangelicol; alloisoimperatorin; 5-methxoy-8-hydroxypsoralen; anomalin; angenomalin; bergaptene; umbelliferone; angelicacid; angelicotoxin.

2. Volatile oils: 3-methylene-6- (1-methylethyl)-cyclohexene; 4, 11, 11-trimethyl-8-methylene bicyclo [7, 2, 0] undec-4-ene; elemene; hexadecanoic acid; 8-nonanoic acid; nonanol; undecane; 10-undecenoic acid; 1-tetradecanol; 1,1-dimethyl, 1, 2-(3-methyl-1, 3-butadiene) cyclopropane; nonyl cyclopropane; tridecanoic acid; 13-methyl pentadecanoic acid.

Angelica dahurica var. formosana

1. Coumarins: isoimperatorin; imperatorin; oxypeucedanin; oxypeucedanin hydrate; bergaptene.

2. Volatile oils: methyl cyclodecane; 1-tetradecene; agidol; ethyllaurate; 9(Z)-octadecen-1-ol; 1-monolinolein; exaltolide; octa-decanol; α-guriunene.

Pharmacological action: Experiments to determine the effects of coumarins on the actions of adrenaline, ACTH, and insulin in fat cells isolated from rats showed that the fucocoumarins oxypeucedanin, bergaprten, imperatorin, and phellopterin activated adrenaline-induced lipolysis. Oxypeucedanin hydrate, imperatorin, and phellopterin also activated ACTH-induced lipolysis, whereas the fucocoumarins byakangelicin, neobyakangelicol and isopimppinellin inhibited insulin-stimulated lipogenesis. Therefore, the roots of *A. Dahurica* activate lipolytic hormones and selectively inhibit antilipolytic hormones.

Attributes: It is pungent in taste and warm in property. Acts on stomach, large intestine and lung meridians.

Action: To dispel wind, remove damp, clear the stuffed nose, and relieve pain, and to promote the subsidence of swelling and drainage of pus.

Indications: Headache, particularly pain in the forehead, and stuffed nose due to colds; sinusitis; toothache; excessive leukorrhea; swelling and pain of sores and wounds.

Dosage: 3-9g.

Storage: Preserve in a cool and dry place, protected from moth.

5.44 Radix Glycyrrhizae (甘草, Gancao)

Liquorice Root

Liquorice root is the dried root and rhizome of *Glycyrrhiza uralensis* Fisch, *Glycyrrhiza inflata* Bat. or *Glycyrrhiza glabra* L. (Fam. Leguminosae). It is collected in spring and autumn, removed from rootlet, and dried in the sun.

Chemical constituents:

Glycyrrhiza uralensis Fisch

1. Triterpenoids: glycyrrhizic acid; 18-β-glycyrrhetic acd; 24-hydroxyglycyrrhetic acid; licoricesaponins A_3, B_2, C_2, D_3, F_3, G_2, H_2, J_2, uralenic acid.

2. Flavonoids: vicenin-2; licoflavone; isolicoflavonol; liquiritigenin; isoliquiritigenin; licochalcone; liquiritigenin-4`-apiosy- (1-2)-glucoside; liquiritigenin-7, 4`-diglucoside; licoricone; ononin; licoricidin; glycyrol; isoglycyrol; glycyrin; glycycoumarin; licoisoflavone; 5-O-mrthyllicoricidin; formononetin.

3. Alkaloids: 5, 6, 7, 8-tetrahydro-2, 4-dimethylquinoline; 5, 6, 7, 8-Tetrahydro-4-methylquinoline.

Glycyrrhiza inflata

1. Triterpenoi*ds:* glycyrrhizic acid; 18-β-glycyrrhetic acid; 11-deoxyglycyrrhetinic acid; methylglycyrrhetate; glycyrrhetic acid acetate; uralsaponin.

2. Flavonoids: licochalcone; licochalcone A; licochalcone C; licoflacone; liquiritigenin; liquiritin; iaoliquiritigenin; formononetin; 4`, 7-dihydroxyflavone; isoliquiritin.

Glycyrrhiza glabra L.

1. Triterpenoids: 18α-hydroxyglycyrrhetic acid; 24-hydroxy-11-deoxyglycyrrhetic acid; 24-hydroxyglycyrrhetic acid; glycyrrhetol; 21α-hydroxyisoglabrolide; liquoric acid.

2. Flavonoids:glabranine; glabrol; liquiritin; liquiritigenin; neoliquiritin; liquiritin-glucorhamnoside; liquiritin-4`-apiosy-(1-2)-glucoside; 3-hydroxyglabrol; licochalcone A; licochalcone B;

isoliquiritin; neoisoliwuiritin; licuraside; rhamnoisoliquiritin; formononetin; 7-acetoxy-2-methylisoflavone; glabrone; glyzaglabrin; glabridin; hispaglabridin A; methoxyglabridin; glabrene; phaseollinisoflaven; hispaglabridin B; 4`-O-methylglabridin.

Pharmacological action: The glycyrrhizin-containing fraction of *Glycyrrhiza* root showed a significant therapeutic effect at oral doses of 200 and 400 mg/kg on chronic gastric ulcers in rats induced by the injection of acetic acid into the gastric wall. The methanolic extract containing glycyrrhizin given intraduodenally inhibited gastric secretion in rats. Glycyrrhetic acid showed mineralocoticoid-like effets and inhibited 5b-reduction of cortisol, aldosterone, and testosterone by rat liver preparation in vitro. Glycyrrhizin could inhibit growth and the cytopathic effects of vaccinia, herpes simplex type 1, Newcastle disease, and vesicular stomatitis virus in cultures of human aneupoid HEP2 cells. Furthermore, glycyrrhizin showed an antiallergic activity.

The flavonoids liquilitigenin, liquiritin, licuroside, and the total flavonoids administered to rats inhibited the passage of Ba_2SO_4 suspension from the stomach into the intestine by reducing stomach motility.

Attributes: It is sweet in taste and mild in property. Acts on heart, lung, spleen and stomach meridians.

Action: To reinforce the function of the spleen and replenish *qi*, remove heat and counteract toxicity, dispel phlegm and relieve cough, alleviate spasmodic pain, and moderate drug actions.

Indications: Weakness of the spleen and the stomach marked by lassitude and weakness; cardiac palpitation and shortness of breath; cough with much phlegm; spasmodic pain in the epigastrium, abdomen and limbs; carbuncles and sores. It is often used for reducing the toxic or drastic actions of other drugs.

Dosage: 1.5-9g.

Storage: Preserve in a ventilated dry place, protected from moth.

5.45 Rhizoma Apiniae Officinarum (高良姜, Gaoliangjiang)

Lesser Galangal Rhizome
Lesser galangal rhizome is the dried rhizome of *Alpinia officinarum* Hance (Fam. Zingiberaceae). It is collected at the end of summer and the

beginning of autumn, removed from fibrous root and remaining leaf scales, washed clean, cut into sections, and dried in the sun.

Chemical constituents:

1. Flavonoids: quercetin; kaempferol; quercetin-3-O-methyl ether; isorhamnetin; kaempferide; galangin; glangin-3-methyl ether; kaempferol-7-methyl ether; 7-hydroxy-3, 5-dimethoxyflavone; alpinin.

2. Diphenylheptanoids: 7-(4``-hydroxyphenyl)-1-phenyl-4-hepten-3-one; 5-hydroxy-1, 7-bis (4-hydroxy-3-methoxyphenyl)-3-heptanone; 5-methoxy-7- (4``-hydroxyphenyl)-1-phenyl-3-heptanone; 5-methoxy-1, 7-diphenyl-3-heptanone; 5-hydroxy-1, 7-diphenyl-3-heptanone; 5-hydroxy-7-(4``-hydroxy-3``-methoxyphenyl)-1-heptanone; (3R, 5R)-1-(4``-hydroxyphenyl)-7-phenylheptane-3, 5-diol; octahydrocurcumin; 1, 7-diphenylhept-4-en-3-one; 7-(4``-hydroxyp-3``-methoxyphenyl)-1-phenylhept-4-en-3-one; 7-(4``-hydroxy-3``-methoxyphenyl)-1-phenyl-3, 5-heptadione; 5-methoxy-7-(4``-hydroxy-3``-methoxyphenyl)-1-phenyl-3-heptanone; 5-hydroxy-7-(4``-hydroxyphenyl)-1-phenyl-3-heptanone.

3. Volatile oils: cineole; methyl cinnanate; α-pinene; eugenol; galangol; cadinene.

4. Others: β-sitosterol; stigmasterol; (6)-zingerol; benzylacetone and eualpinol.

Pharmacological action: The new diarylheptanoids isolated from *A. officinarum* were found to exhibit an inhibitory activity on prostaglandin biosynthesis.

Attributes: It is pungent in taste and hot in property. Acts on spleen and stomach meridians.

Action: To dispel cold from the stomach, to promote digestion and to relieve pain.

Indications: Epigastric pain with cold sensation; vomiting, belching and acid regurgitation due to cold in the stomach.

Dosage: 3-6g.

Storage: Preserve in a cool and dry place.

5.46 Rhizoma Dioscoreae (山药， Shanyao)

Common Yam Rhizome

Common yam rhizome is the dried rhizome of *Dioscorea opposita* Thunb. (Fam. Dioscoreaceae). It is collected in winter when the stem and leaf are withered, deprived of root stock, washed clean and deprived of outer bark and fibrous root, fumigated with sulfur, and then dried.

Chemical constituents: Diosgenin; cholide; d-abscinin; vitamin C; 3, 4-dihydroxy-phenylethylamine; mannan and phytic acid.

Pharmacological action: In male Wistar rats fed diets containing diosgenin, the secretion of biliary chresterol, bile salt, and phospholipid was investigated. The theoretical maximal biliary cholesterol output significantly increase by 500 percent in diosgenin-fed animals.

Attributes: It is sweet in taste and mild in property. Acts on spleen, lung and kidney meridians.

Action: To replenish the spleen and stomach, promote fluid secretion and benefit the lung, and to strengthen the kidney and restrain seminal discharge.

Indications: Anorexia and chronic diarrhea due to diminished function of the spleen; cough and dyspnea due to diminished function of the lung; seminal emission, excessive leukorrhea, frequency of urination or diabetes due to deficiency condition of the kidney.

Dosage: 15-30g.

Storage: Preserve in a ventilated dry place, protected from moth.

5.47 Rhizoma Imperatae (白茅根， Baimaogen)

Lalang Grass Rhizome

Lalang grass rhizome is the fresh rhizome of *Imperata cylindrica* Beauv. *var. major* (Nees) C.E. Hubb. (Fam. Gramineae). It is collected in spring and autumn, washed clean, removed from fibrous root and membranous leaf sheath, and tied up in a small bundle.

Chemical constituents: Glucose, fructose, xylose, sucrose, anemonin

Pharmacological action: The decoction of the herb showed antiseptic, antiviral diuretic and hemostatic activities.

Attributes: It is sweet in taste and cold in property. Acts on lung, stomach and bladder meridians.

Action: To arrest bleeding by reducing heat in blood, to remove heat, and to cause diuresis.

Indications: Spitting of blood, epistaxis and hematuria due to heat in the blood; febrile diseases with thirst; jaundice; urinary infection with difficult painful urination; edema in acute nephritis.

Dosage: 30-60g.

Storage: Preserve in a cool place, protected from moth.

5.48 Rhizoma Phragmitis (芦根，Lugen)

Reed Rhizome

Reed rhizome is the fresh rhizome of *Phragmites communis* Trin. (Fam. Gramineae). It is collected all the year round, washed clean, removed from buds, fibrous root and membranaceous leaf.

Chemical constituents: Carbohydrates, polyols, betaine, tricin, vitamin B_1, B_2 and C

Pharmacological action: The decoction of the herb showed antiviral activity.

Attributes: It is sweet in taste and cold in property. Acts on lung and stomach meridians.

Action: To remove heat, promote the production of body fluid, relieve emesis, and alleviate dysuria.

Indications: Dire thirst in febrile diseases; vomiting or retching due to heat in the stomach; heat in the lung with cough; lung abscess; urinary infection with difficult painful urination.

Dosage: 30-60g.

Storage: Preserve in wet sand, protected from moth.

5.49 Rhizoma Zingiberis Recens (生姜，Shengjiang)

Fresh Ginger

Fresh ginger is the fresh rhizome of *Zingiber officinale* (Willd.) Rosc. (Fam. Zingiberaceae). It is collected in autumn and winter, removed from fibrous root and soil.

Chemical constituents: 2-heptanol; 1, 3, 3-trimethyltricyclo [2, 2, 1, 0] heptane; tricyclene; α-pinene; β-frenchene; β-pinene, 6-methyl-5-hepten-2-one; myrcene; octanal, α-thujene; $\Delta^{1(7)}$-menthene; 1, 3, 3-trimethyl-2-oxybicylclo [2, 2, 2] octane; nonyl alcohol; 4-methyl-1-(1-methylethyl)-3-cyclohexen-1-ol-acetate; 2-nonanone; fenchyl alcohol; citronellol; isofenchyl alcohol; Δ^3-menthene; citral (Z); citral (E); safrole; geraniol; methyl-eugenol; (*E*)- β-farnesene; 1-(1, 5-dimethyl-4-hexenyl)-4-methylbenzene; 2, 6-dimethyl-6-(4-methyl-3-pentenyl)biscyclo(3, 1, 1)hept-2-ene; α-farnesene; (Z)-β-farnesene; 1R-(1α,3α,4β)-4-ethenyl-2, 2, 4-trimethyl-3-(1-methylethyl)cyclohexane-mathanol; nerolidol; farnesol; nerol(Z); *n*-heptane; *n*-octane; *n*-nonane; acetaldehyde; propionaldehyde; acetone; methyl isobutyl ketone; glyoxal; methylglyoxal; n-propanol; *sec*-butanol; *tert*-butanol; *n*-nonanol; diethyl sulfide; methyl allyl sulfide; methylacetate; ethyl acetate; methyl acetate;

camphene; sabinene; Δ^3-carene ;limonene; β-phellandrene; 1, 8-cineole; p-cymene; r-terpinene; terpinolene; linalool; perillal; camphor; isoborneol; borneol; terpinen-4-ol; α-terpineol; terpinen-4-ol; α-terpineol; neral; geranial; bornyl acetate; citronellyl acetate; α-cubebene; geranyl acetate; α-copaene; β-elemene; β-caryophyllene; r-elemene; α-bergamotene; trans-β-farnesene; alloaromadendrene; α-curcumene; α-zingiberene; β-bisabolene; β-santalol; E-nerolidol; farnesol; elemol; β-eudesmol; zinggiberol; Z-nerolidol; zonarene; cis-β-sesquiphellandrol; trans-β-sesquiphellandrol; 3-caraneol; 2-caraneol; 2-borneol; b-cedrene; zingerone; 1-(4-hydroxy-3-methoxyphenyl)-3, 5-octanediol; 6-gingediol; 8-gingediol; 10-gingediol; 6-methylgingediol; 1-(4-hydroxy-3-methoxyphenyl)-3, 5-diacetoxyoctane; 6-gingediacetate; 6-methylgingediacetate; 4-gingerol; 6-gingerol; 6-gingerdione; 10-gingerdione; 6-dehydrogingerdione; 10- dehydrogingerdione; 6-shogaol; gingerenone A, B; isogingerenone B; gingerenone C; meso-3, 5-diacetoxy-1, 7-bis(4-hydroxy-3-methoxyphenyl)heptane; 3, 5-diacetoxy-1-(4-hydroxy-3, 5-diacetoxyphenyl)-7-(4-hydroxy-3-methoxyphenyl)-heptane; glanolactone; (E)-8β, 17-epoxylabd-12-ene-15, 16-dial.

Pharmacological action: The methanolic extract of ginger rhizome or its active ingredients showed significantly antipyretic analgesic, inotropic and antihepatotoxic activities, and possess potent inhibitory effects on prostaglandin biosynthesis

Attributes: It is pungent in taste and slight warm in property. Acts on lung, spleen and stomach meridians.

Action: To induce perspiration and dispel cold, warm the stomach and arrest vomiting, and resolve phlegm and relieve cough.

Indications: Common cold; vomiting caused by cold in the stomach; cough with expectoration of whitish thin sputum.

Dosage: 3-9g.

Storage: Preserve in a cool, dry place, or embed in wet sand, protected from freezing.

5.50 Semen Armeniacae Amarum (杏仁， Xingren)

Apricot Seed

Apricot seed is the dried ripe seed of *Prunus armeniaca* L. var. *ansu* Maxim., *Prunus sibirica* L., *Prunus mandshurica* (Maxim.) Koehne or *Prunus armeniaca* L. (Fam. Rosaceae). The fruit is collected in summer and it is removed from the pulp and the shell, and dried in the sun.

Chemical constituents:
1. Glycoside: amygdamin.
2. Fatty acids: oleic acid; linoleic acid; palmitic acid; stearic acid; linolenic acid; tetradecanoic acid; palmitoleic acid; eicosenoic acid.
3. Volatile oils: β-ionone; linalool; γ-decanolactone; hexanal; (E)-2-hexenal; (E, E)-2, 4-decadienal; (E)-2-nonenal; γ-dodecalactone; α-terpineol; geraniol.

Pharmacological action: The decoction of this food and amygdalin showed antitussive, antasthmatic, cancer-preventive and antiinflammatory activities

Attributes: It is bitter in taste and slight warm in property. Acts on lung and large intestine meridians.

Action: To relieve cough and asthma, and to relax bowels.

Indications: Cough and asthma accompanied by stuffiness in the chest and profuse expectoration; constipation due to deficiency of blood and fluid.

Dosage: 4.5-9g.

Storage: Preserve in a cool and dry place, protected from moth.

5.51 Semen Canavaliae (刀豆，Daodou)

Jack Bean

Jack bean is the dried ripe seed of *Canavalia gladiata* (Jacg.) DC. (Fam. Leguminosae). The fruit is collected in autumn when ripe, and it is gathered, and dried in the sun.

Chemical constituents: Acacetin; apigenin; isorhamnetin; kaempferol; luteolin; quercetin; canavanine; atachylose.

Pharmacological action: The decoction of the food possesses cancer-preventive and antiviral activities.

Attributes: It is bitter in taste and slight warm in property. Acts on lung and large intestine meridians.

Action: To relieve cough and asthma, and to relax bowels.

Indications: Cough and asthma accompanied by stuffiness in the chest and profuse expectoration; constipation due to deficiency of blood and fluid.

Dosage: 4.5-9g.

Storage: Preserve in a cool and dry place, protected from moth.

5.52 Semen Cassiae (决明子, Juemingzi)

Cassia Seed

Cassia seed is the dried ripe seed of *Cassia obtusifolia* L. or *Cassia tora* L. (Fam. Leguminosae). The ripe legume is collected in autumn and dried in the sun, it is tapped out and foreign matter removed.

Chemical constituents:

1. Anthraquinone derivates: chrysophanol; emodin; aloe-emodin; rhein; emodin-6-glucoside; emodin anthrone; physcion; obtusin; obtusifolin; aurantio-obtusin; chrysophanol-1-β-gentiobioside; chrysophanic acid-9-anthrone; 1-[(β-D-glucopyranosyl-(1-3)-O- β -D-glucopyranosyl-(1-6)-O-β-D-glucopyranosyl)oxy]-8-hydroxy-3-methyl-9, 10-anthraquinone; 1-[(β-D-glucopyranosyl-(1-6)-O-β-D-glucopyranosyl-(1-3)-O-β-D-glucopyranosyl)oxy]-8-hydroxy-3-methyl-9, 10-anthraquinone; 2-(β-D-glucopyranosyloxy)-8-hydroxy-3-methyl-9, 10-anthraqui none.

2. Naphthopyranone derivates: rubrofusarin; nor-rubrofusarin; cassiaside; torachrysone; toralactone; rubrofusarin-6-β-gentiobioside; 9-[(β-D-glucopyranosyl-(1-6)-O-β-D-glucopyranosyl)oxy]-10-hydroxy-7-methoxy-3-methyl-1H-naphtho[2, 3-C] pyran-1-one; 6-[(α-apifuranosyl-(1-6)-O-β-D-glucopyranosyl)oxy-rubrofusarin.

Pharmacological action: The decoction and methanolic extract of *Cassia obtusifolia* L. or *Cassia tora* L. showed significant inhibitory effects on hyperlipemia and hypertentsion. Also, the methanolic extracts possess marked antiseptic immunoregulatory activities.

Attributes: It is sweet, bitter and salty in taste and slight cold in property. Acts on liver and large intestine meridians.

Action: To remove heat from the liver, improve eyesight and relax bowels.

Indications: Inflammation of the eye with pain, photophobia and lacrimination; headache, dizziness, blurred vision and constipation.

Dosage: 9-15g.

Storage: Preserve in a dry place.

5.53 Semen Coicis (薏苡仁, Yiyiren)

Coix Seed

Coix seed is the dried ripe kernel of *Coix lacrymajobi* L. var. Ma-yuen (Roman.) Stapf (Fam. Gramineae). The plant is collected in autumn when the fruit is ripe and dried in the sun. The fruit is picked up, dried in the sun, and the kernel is separated from the shell, a yellowish-brown coat, and foreign matter.

Chemical constituents: Coixenolide; coixol; feruloyl stigmasterol; feruloyl campesterol; coixan A, B, C; 4-ketopinoresinol.

Pharmacological action: The ethanol extract of the food and coixenolide showed significant antiplastic, anti-inflammatory, immunoregulatory and sedative activities. Coixan A, B, C showed hypoglycemic activity.

Attributes: It is sweet in taste and cool in property. Acts on spleen, stomach and lung meridians.

Action: To invigorate the spleen function and promote diuresis, alleviate arthritis, arrest diarrhea, remove heat and facilitate the drainage of pus.

Indications: Edema, oliguria; arthritis with contracture of joints; diarrhea due to to diminished function of the spleen; lung abscess, appendicitis; verruca plana..

Dosage: 9-30g.

Storage: Preserve in a ventilated dry place, protected from moth.

5.54 Semen Euryales (芡实， Qianshi)

Gordon Euryale Seed

Gordon Euryale seed is the dried ripe kernel of *Euryale ferox* Salisb. (Fam. Nymphaeaceae). The ripe fruits is collected in late autumn and early winter and peeled; it is taken out, washed, removed from the hard shell, and dried.

Chemical constituents: Vitamin C, thiamine, riboflavine.

Pharmacological action: The decoction of the food showed diuretic activity.

Attributes: It is sweet in taste and mild in property. Acts on spleen and kidney meridians.

Action: To benefit the kidney and arrest seminal discharge, to invigorate the function of the spleen and relieve diarrhea, and to remove damp and check excessive leukorrhea.

Indications: Nocturnal emission, spermatorrhea, enuresis, frequent urination; chronic diarrhea due to hypofunction of the spleen; turbid discharge mixed with urine, excessive leukorrhea.

Dosage: 9-15g.

Storage: Preserve in a ventilated dry place, protected from moth.

5.55 Semen Ginkgo (白果， Baiguo)

Ginkgo Seed

Ginkgo seed is the dried ripe seed of *Ginkgo biloba* L. (Fam. Ginkgoaceae). It is collected in autumn when ripe, removed from the fleshy test, washed clean, steamed or boiled briefly, and dried by baking gently.

Chemical constituents:

1. Flavonoids: kaempferol; kaempferol-3-O-rhamnoside; heptaacetyl kaempferol glucoside; kaempferol-3- (6``-ρ-coumaroyl-glucoside)-β-1, 4-rhamnoside; quercetin; isorhamnetin; octaacetyl quercetin glucoside; rutin; heptaacetyl luteolin glucoside; octaacetyl dephidenon glucoside; (+)-catechin-pentaacetate; (-)-epicatechin-pentaacetate; (+)-gallocatechin-hexacetate; (-)-epigallocatechin-hexaacetate; bilobetin; ginkgetin; sciadopitysin; 1, 5`-methoxy-bilobetin.

2. Organic acids and alcohols: ginkgolic acid; hydroginkgolic acid; ginkgolinic acid; ginkgol; bilobol; quinic acid; linoleic acid; shikimic acid; asorbic acid; α-hexenol; sequoyitol; pinite; hexacosanol; octacosanol-1; nonacosyl alcohol; ginnol.

Pharmacological action: Bilobol showed an inhibitory effect on hypertension.

Attributes: It is sweet and bitter in taste and mild in property. Acts on lung meridian.

Action: To arrest persistent cough and asthma, and to reduce leukorrhea and urination.

Indications: Persistent cough and asthma with profuse expectoration; morbid leukorrhea with whitish discharge; enuresis, frequent urination.

Dosage: 4.5-9g.

Storage: Preserve in a ventilated dry place.

5.56 Semen Lablab Album (白扁豆， Baibiandou)

White Hyacinth Bean

White hyacinth bean is the dried ripe seed of *Dolichos lablab* L. (Fam. Leguminosae). The fruit is collected in autumn and winter when ripe, dried in the sun, and it is gathered, and dried again in the sun.

Chemical constituents: stigmasterol; trigonelline; 3-O-β-D-glucopyranosyl-gibberellin A, sucrose; glucose; galacose; fructose.

Pharmacological action: The decoction of the food showed antiviral and antibacterial activities.

Attributes: It is sweet in taste and slight warm in property. Acts on spleen and stomach meridians.

Action: To invigorate the spleen and remove damp, particularly the summer damp.

Indications: Weakness of the spleen and stomach with loss of appetite and loose bowels; excessive leukorrhea; vomiting, diarrhea, distress in the chest and distension in the abdomen caused by summer-damp.

Dosage: 9-15g.

Storage: Preserve in a dry place, protected from moth.

5.57 Semen Myristicae (肉豆蔻，Roudoukou)

Nutmeg

Nutmeg is the dried kernel of *Myristica fragrans* Houtt (Fam.Myristicaceae).

Chemical constituents:

1. Volatile oils: β-pinene; terpinen-4-ol; safrole; methyl eugenol; myristicin; elemicin; d-camphene; α-pinene; myristic acid.

2. Phenylpropanoids: licarin B; 2-(4-allyl-2, 6-dimethoxyphenyl)-4-hydroxy-3-methoxyphenylpropan-1-ol; fragransol, A, B, C; myristicanol A, B; fragransin A_1, A_2, B_1, B_2, B_3, C_1, C_2, C_{3a}, C_{3b}, D_1, D_2, D_3, E_1.

Pharmacological action: The decoction of this food could be utilized for insomnia and indigestion. Its volatile oil possesses significant antibacterial and antifungal actions.

Attributes: It is pungent in taste and warm in property. Acts on spleen, stomach and large intestine meridians.

Action: To warm the spleen and stomach and promote the flow of *qi*, to arrest diarrhea as an astringent.

Indications: Deficiency-cold of the spleen and stomach with persistent diarrhea, epigastric and abdominal distension and pain, anorexia, and vomiting.

Dosage: 3-9g.

Storage: Preserve in a cool and dry place, protected from moth.

5.58 Semen Nelumbinis (莲子，Lianzi)

Lotus Seed

Lotus seed is the dried ripe seed of *Nelumbo nucifera* Gaertn. (Fam. Nymphaceae). It is collected in autumn when the fruit is ripe, removed from the pericarp, and dried.

Chemical constituents: nuciferine; N-nornuciferine; pronuciferine; neferine; liensinine; isoliensinine; oxoushinsunine; nornuciferine; N-methylasimilobine; anonaine; roemerine; armepavine; N-norarmepavine; asimilobine; lirinidine; higenamine; quercetin; rutin; hyperin.

Pharmacological action: Nuciferine had depressant properties on the CNS in rodents, as well as weak anti-inflammatory, analgetic, antitussive, antiserotonin, and adrenergic blocking activities.

Attributes: It is sweet in taste and mild in property. Acts on spleen, kidney and heart meridians.

Action: To tonify the spleen, to relieve diarrhea, to replenish the kidney, to arrest seminal emission, and to nourish the heart, to induce tranquilization.

Indications: Protracted diarrhea due to hypofunction of the spleen, seminal emission, leukorrhagia; palpitation, insomnia.

Dosage: 6-15g.

Storage: Preserve in a dry place, protected from moth.

5.59   Semen Persicae (桃仁， Taoren)

Peach Seed

Peach seed is the dried ripe seed of *Prunus persica* (L.) Batsch or *Prunus davidiana* (Carr.) Franch. (Fam. Rosaceae). The fruit is collected when ripe. It is removed from sarcocarp and shell, and dried in the sun.

Chemical constituents: Triacyl glycerol; 1,2-biacyl glycerol; 1, 3-biacyl glycerol; monoacyl glycerol; 24-methylenecylortanol; (+)-catechin; prunin; hesperetin-5-O-glucoside naringerin; dihydro-kaempferol; kaempferide; quercetin glucoside; sucrose; amygdalin, prunasin; glucose.

Pharmacological action: The decoction of the food showed marked antihypertensive, laxative, diuretic, antitussive, antibacterial, antioxidative, antiplastic, hepato-preventive activities.

Attributes: It is bitter and sweet in taste and mild in property. Acts on heart, liver and large intestine meridians.

Action: To promote blood circulation, eliminate phlegm and relax the bowels.

Indications: Amenorrhea, dysmenorrhea, mass formation in the abdomen, traumatic injuries; constipation.

Dosage: 4.5-9g.

Storage: Preserve in a cool and dry place, protected from moth.

5.60 Semen Phaseoli (赤小豆， Chixiaodou)

Rice Bean

Rice bean is the dried ripe seed of *Phaseolus calcaratus* Roxb. Or*Phaseolus angularis* Wight (Fam. Leguminosae). It is collected when the fruit is ripe, and dried in the sun.

Chemical constituents: Proteins; saccharides; thiamine; riboflavine; nicitic acid.

Pharmacological action: The decoction of the food showed antibacterial and immunoregulatory activities.

Attributes: It is sweet and sour in taste and mild in property. Acts on heart and small intestine meridians.

Action: To cause diuresis, to counteract toxicity, and to promote the drainage of pus.

Indications: Edema; jaundice with dark urine; acute rheumatic arthritis; carbuncles, boils, appendicitis.

Dosage: 9-30g.

Storage: Preserve in a dry place, protected from moth.

5.61 Semen Pruni (郁李仁， Yuliren)

Chinese Dwarf Cherry Seed

Chinese dwarf cherry seed is the dried ripe seed of *Prunus humilis* Bge., *Prunus japonica* Thunb. or *Prunus pedunculata* Maxim. (Fam. Rosaceae). The ripe fruit is collected in summer and autumn, removed from the sarcocarp and the shells and dried.

Chemical constituents:

1. Flavonoids: afzelin; kaempferitrin; multiflorin; multinoside; prunuside.

2. Organic acids: ursolic acid; vanillic acid; protocatechuic acid, oleic acid.

3. Others: amygalin.

Pharmacological action: The decoction of the food showed laxative, antitussive and antiinflammatory activities.

Attributes: It is pungent, bitter and sweet in taste and mild in property. Acts on spleen, large intestine and small intestine meridians.

Action: To relax the bowels, and to cause diuresis.

Indications: Stagnancy of undigested food with abdominal distension and constipation; weakness and edema of the legs with oliguria.

Dosage: 3-9g.

Storage: Preserve in a cool and dry place, protected from moth.

5.62 Semen Raphani (莱菔子， Laifuzi)

Radish Seed

Radish seed is the dried ripe seed of *Raphanus sativus* L. (Fam. Cruciferae). It is collected in summer when the fruit is ripe, and the seed is rubbed out, and dried in the sun.

Chemical constituents: biotin, *S*-carboxymethylcystein, 3, 22, 23-trihydroxystigmatstan-6-one.

Pharmacological action: It showed anti-tussive activity and was utilized for the treatment of indigestion.

Attributes: It is pungent and sweet in taste and mild in property. Acts on lung, spleen and stomach meridians.

Action: To promote digestion and relieve abdominal distension, and to relieve cough and resolve phlegm.

Indications: Retention of undigested food with epigastric and abdominal distension and pain, and constipation; diarrhea due to stagnation of undigested food; cough and dyspnea with copious expectoration.

Dosage: 4.5-9g.

Storage: Preserve in a ventilated dry place, protected from moth.

5.63 Semen Sesami Nigrum (黑芝麻， Heizhima)

Black Sesame

Black sesame is the dried ripe seed of *Sesamum indicum* L. (Fam. Pedaliaceae). The plant is collected in autumn when the fruit is ripe, and dried in the sun. It is gathered, foreign matter removed, and dried in the sun.

Chemical constituents: Fatty oils; α-glubolin; β-glubolin; ^{13}S-glubolin; albumin; amino acids; sesamin; sesamol; sesamolin; β-sitosterol; campesterol; stigmasterol; glucose; galactose; fructose; sucrose; sesamose; lecithin; nicotinic acid; riboflavin; vitamin B_6; vitamin E; vitamin C; cytochrome C and pedaliin.

Pharmacological action: It showed anti-aging and antiadrenergic activities, and could be utilized for the treatment of hyperglycemia.

Attributes: It is sweet in taste and mild in property. Acts on liver, kidney and large intestine meridians.

Action: To tonify the liver and the kidney, to replenish vital essence and blood, and to relax the bowels.

Indications: Dizziness, blurred vision, tinnitus, impaired hearing, premature greying of the hair and beard; loss of hair after a serious disease; constipation..

Dosage: 9-15g.

Storage: Preserve in a ventilated dry place, protected from moth.

5.64 Semen Brassicae Junceae (黄芥子，Huangjiezi)

Yellow Mustard Seed

Yellow mustard seed is the dried ripe seed of *Brassica juncea* (L.) Czern. et Coss. (Fam. Cruciferae). The plant is cut up in late summer and early autumn when the fruit is ripe, and dried in the sun. It is tapped out and foreign matter removed.

Chemical constituents: gluconapin; 4-hydroxy-3-indolymethyl glucosinolate; glucobrassicin; neoglucobrassicin; progoitrin; myrosin; sinapic acid; sinapine.

Pharmacological action: The food showed antitussive and antiasthmatic acivities.

Attributes: It is pungent in taste and warm in property. Acts on lung meridian.

Action: To relieve dyspnea and cough by eliminating cold-phlegm, to reduce nodulation, and to relieve pain by removing the obstruction of collaterals.

Indications: Cough, asthma and distending pain of the chest caused by cold-phlegm; arthralgia accompanied by numbness due to obstruction of collaterals by phlegm; deep abscess.

Dosage: 3-9g.

Storage: Preserve in a ventilated dry place, protected from moisture.

5.65 Semen Sojae Preparatum (淡豆豉，Dandouchi)

Fermented Soybean

Fermented soybean is the fermented preparation obtained from the ripe seed of *Glycine max* (L.) Merr. (Fam. Leguminosae).

Chemical constituents: acetopine; N-γ-glutamyltyrosine; glyceolin; 6a-hydroxyphasellin; N-(1H-indol-3-ylacetyl)-aspartic acid; N-(1H-indol-3-ylacetyl)-glutamic acid; 12-oleanene-3, 21, 22, 24-tetrol; soyasaponin A, B, C, D, E, F, G, I, II, III, IV, V.

Attributes: It is bitter and pungent in taste and cool in property. Acts on lung and stomach meridians.

Action: To induce diaphoresis, to ease the mind, and to relieve fever.

Indications: Chills, fever and headache in colds and influenza; vexation, oppressed feeling in the chest and insomnia.

Dosage: 6-12g.

Storage: Preserve in a ventilated dry place, protected from moth.

5.66 Semen Torreyae (榧子, Feizi)

Grand Torreya Seed

Grand torreya seed is the dried ripe seed of *Torreya grandis* Fort. (Fam.Taxaceae). It is collected in autumn when ripe, removed from the fleshy aril, washed clean, and dried in the sun.

Chemical constituents: linoleic acid; stearic acid; oleic acid; gliadin; palmitic acid; behenic acid; lauric acid; myristic acid; torreyagrandate,torreyaflavone and torreyaflavonoloside.

Pharmacological action: It showed taeniacidal, lumbricidal and trypanosomicidal activities and is used for the treatment of ancylostomiasis.

Attributes: It is sweet in taste and mild in property. Acts on lung, stomach and large intestine meridians.

Action: To kill worms and to relax bowels.

Indications: Ankylostomiasis, ascariasis, taeniasis; abdominal pain and malnutrition caused by intestinal parasitosis in children; constipation.

Dosage: 9-15g.

Storage: Preserve in a cool and dry place, protected from moth.

5.67 Semen Ziziphi Spinosae (酸枣仁, Suanzaoren)

Spine Date Seed

Spine date seed is the dried ripe seed of *Ziziphus jujuba* Mill. *Var. spinosa* (Bunge) Hu ex H. F. Chou (Fam. Taxaceae). The ripe fruit is collected in later autumn and early winter. It is is collected and removed from the pulp and shell, and dried in the sun.

Chemical constituents:

    1 Triterpenoids: betulic acid; betulin; jujuboside A, B, B_1 and jujubogenin.

2 Flavonoids: swertisin; zivulgarin; spinosin; $2^{``}$-O-β-D-glucopyranosylawertisin; $6^{```}$-O-sinapoyl-spinosin; $6^{```}$-O-feruloylspinosin; $6^{```}$-O-ρ-coumaroylspinosin.
3. Others: vitamin C, ferulic acid.

Pharmacological action: The flavone C-glycosides swertisin, spinosin, and acylspinosins were found to exhibit sedative activity in animal experiments. Of the flavonoids, swertisin showed highest sedative activity.

Attributes: It is sweet and sour in taste and mild in property. Acts on liver, gall-bladder and heart meridians.

Action: To replenish the liver, to tranquilize, to arrest excessive perspiration, and to promote the production of body fluid.

Indications: Insomnia, dream-disturbed sleep; excessive sweating due to debility; thirst due to consumption of body fluid.

Dosage: 9-15g.

Storage: Preserve in a cool and dry place, protected from moth.

5.68 Thallus Laminariae (昆布， Kunbu)

Kelp or Tangle

Kelp or tangle is the dried thalline of *Laminaria japonica* Aresch. (Fam. Laminariaceae) or *Ecklonia kurome* Okam. (Fam. Alariaceae). It is collected in summer and autumn, and dried in the sun.

Chemical constituents: algin; laminarin; alginic acid; fucoidin; laminine; thiamine; riboflavine, vitamin C; eckol; 2-O-(2, 4, 6-trihydroxyphenyl)-6, $6^`$-bieckol; 2-O-(2, 4, 6-trihydroxyphenyl)-8, $8^`$-bieckol; phlorofucofuroeckol A; fucan sulfate; fucan sulfate B-I; B-II, C-I and C-II.

Pharmacological action: The decoction of the food showed significant antiplastic, immonoregulatory and antiasthmatic activities. It was often used for the treatment of hyperglycemia, hyperlipidemia and hypertension.

Attributes: It is salty in taste and cold in property. Acts on liver, stomach and kidney meridians.

Action: To eliminate phlegm, soften hard masses and dissolve lumps, and to cause diuresis.

Indications: Goiter, scrofula, swelling and pain of the testes; edema.

Dosage: 6-12g.

Storage: Preserve in a dry place.

5.69 Zaocys (乌梢蛇, Wushaoshe)

Black Snake

Black snake is the dried body of *Zaocys dhumnades* (Cantor) (Fam. Laminariaceae). It is collected in summer and autumn, opened in the abdomen or opened after the skin is stripped except the head and tail skin, removed from the viscera, coiled up in disc-shape and dried.

Chemical constituents: arginine; phenylalanine; tyrosine; isoleucine; glutamic acid; threonine; histidine and cholic acid.

Pharmacological action: The alcohol extract of the food showed significant anti-inflammatory, sedative and analgesic activities.

Attributes: It is sweet in taste and mild in property. Acts on liver meridian.

Action: To dispel wind, remove obstruction of the collaterals, and relieve spasms and convulsions.

Indications: Chronic rheumatiod arthritis with numbness and ankylosis; hemiplegia in stroke; convulsion, tetanus, leprosy, scabies, scrofula with suppuration.

Dosage: 9-12g.

Storage: Preserve in a dry place, protected from mould and moth.

Chapter 6
Application of Chinese Functional Food

6.1 For Maintaining Health

Maintaining health includes improving looks, controlling weight, promoting intelligence, building up strength, improving vision, clear hearing and beautiful hair, dental health, and so on.

6.1.1 Improving Looks
The theory of TCM holds that a person's complexion and appearance indicate their state of health. A normal or abnormal look reflects their condition. A sickly look, in fact, is an imbalance of *yin, yang, qi* and blood of the body. Therefore, if you would like to keep your face youthful or treat a disease of the face, you first have to adjust or regulate the function of *yin, yang, qi* and blood of *zang-fu* of the body in order to make them balance.

The theory of TCM maintains that the spleen dominates the muscle, the lung dominates the skin and hair, the heart controls the blood and vessels, the kidney is the congenital vital foundation, etc. Thus, the functional food to improve looks is always used to adjust the function of *zang-fu* mentioned above.

The principle of improving looks in TCM is different from the Western nutritional medicine. A doctor in Western nutritional medicine will always notice the face. When a person gets on in years, his face begins to wrinkle. So the doctors suggest that the person had better use a powder compact to make up her face, or use some other drugs just like a powder compact. Also, if the countenance of a person is unhealthy or if he has a skin disease on face, the Western doctors always treats the face, they do not pay attention to other organs. But the Chinese doctors are different. They examine the possible problem in other organs.

Which foods have the function of improving looks? Fresh bamboo shoots, sea cucumber, rape, dried shrimp, fingered citron, soft-shelled turtle, the leaves of Chinese toon, bean curd, soybean, peach blossom, pineapple, apple, spinach, golden orange, orange, rose, etc. These foods can be cooked in Chinese functional food.

Stewed Sea Cucumber with Fresh Bamboo Shoots

Process: Take 200g of sea cucumber, which have already been soaked in warm water and expanded. Cut them into strips. Clean 100g fresh bamboo shoots and cut into pieces. Put them into a pan, then add 500ml pork soup and simmer until done. Add salt, sugar, soy source, yellow wine and starch. Serve when it becomes soup.

Fried Rape with Dried Shrimp

Process: Wash 200g rape and cut into strips. Stir-fry the rape, then add 50g dried shrimp which have been soaked in warm water. Add salt, sugar, MSG and some chicken soup. Mix starch when it is done. The soup looks very clear.

Fingered Citron and Bamboo Shoots

Process: Wash 200g fresh bamboo shoots and cut into pieces. Wash 20g fingered citron and 10g ginger, cut into slices. Put into an earthenware pot, then add water, and bring to boil. Add salt, MSG, mix and stir evenly, steeping for 24 hours in the pot before serving.

Herba Artemisiae Chinghao and Soft-Shelled Turtle Soup

Process: Clean one soft-shelled turtle (about 1,000g). Remove viscera, clean and cut into pieces. Place in a covered casserole dish, add 20g of cut up Herba Artemisiae Chinghao, some water, a little salt, wine, and cook over a low heat until done.

The Leaves of Chinese Toon and Bean Curd in Mixed Sauce

Process: Wash 100g fresh leaves of Chinese toon (or salt leaves soaked in the water), cut into pieces or powder, add bean curd, salt, MSG, sesame oil, mix well and serve.

Fried Purslane and Soy Bean Sprouts

Process: Wash 100g fresh Purslane and cut into strips. Stir-fry soy bean sprouts with vegetable oil, add a little water, bring to boil till almost done, then add Purslane, mix in a little salt, MSG, and a little starch. When the dish is done, pour a little sesame oil over it, remove from the heat and serve.

6.1.2   Reducing Weight

The theory of TCM holds that the cause of fat is "wetness," "phlegm," "phlegm-retention" and "retention of the fluid in the body," etc. The manifestations are lassitude, exhaustion, shortness of breath, palpitations, rapid respiration, and hypersomnia, sluggishness, etc. TCM holds that the lung is in charge of qi; the spleen controls the transportation of wetness; the kidney is the congenital vital foundation; the triple burners or the three portions of the body cavity is the tunnel of water, etc. Therefore, the principle of weight-reducing is to ventilate and smooth the lung and resolve phlegm, invigorate the spleen and remove the dampness through diuresis, and warm the kidney in order to relieve the water retention. Following are some examples.

Fried Crowndaisy Chrysanthemum and Radish

Process: Wash 200g white radish, 100g crowndaisy chrysanthemum, and cut into strips. Pour 100g oil into a pot. When the oil is hot, add wild pepper. When the wild pepper turns black, remove it, then add the radish strips. Add a little chicken soup until almost tender, then the crowndaisy chrysanthemum. Add MSG, salt to taste, mix in starch when the dish is done and pour a little sesame oil over it. Remove from the heat and serve.

Fried Mutton with Wild Pepper and Onions

Process: Pour 50g peanut oil into a pot, and heat over a flame. Add little wild pepper, 200g mutton shreds, 10g ginger shreds, 100g onions, and fry. Add salt, gourmet powder, vinegar, and yellow wine to taste.

Weight-Reducing Wine

Process: Wash 1,000g polished glutinous rice, 150g of seeds of Job's tears, the powder of lotus seeds (about 50g), 100g Chinese yam powder, 50g seeds of gorgon euryale, 50g powder of Poria. Mix well and put into a vessel and add water. Steam for one hour, cool, and mix in baking wine.

Place the vessel in a warm place (25 degrees Centigrade) for 36 to 48 hours.

Ginseng, Pilose Asiabell Root,
Shred-Chicken and Winter Melon Soup

Process: Pluck and eviscerate one chicken and clean it. Cut 200g chicken meat into shreds, add ginseng and Pilose Asiabell Root, 3g each. Place in a covered casserole pot and add 500ml water. Cook over a low heat until the chicken is tender. Then add winter melon pieces (about 200g). Mix in salt, yellow rice wine, a little MSG. Serve when the winter melon is done.

Sauted Bean Sprouts with Lotus Seeds and Lotus

Process: Wash 200g fresh lotus leaves (or dried lotus leaves), and 150g lotus seeds that have been soaked in warm water. Put them into a pot, add some water, and boil to soup. Cut 100g fresh lotus into pieces. Fry until seven-tenths done, add lotus seeds and bean sprouts. Pour some soup of the lotus leaves and seeds, mix in salt, MSG to taste, add a little starch and remove from the heat and serve.

Water-Melon, Winter-Melon and Cucumber
Peel Soaked with Salt

Process: Wash 200g watermelon peel, 300g winter melon, and 400g cucumber peel (remove the seeds). Pour some water over them and boil separately over different heat. Cool and cut into strips. Place them in a vessel, soak for 12 hours with salt, add gourmet powder before using.

6.1.3 Promoting Intelligence

The meaning of promoting intelligence is to strengthen the ability to think and to remember. The relationship between nutrition and intelligence is a subject that nutritionists pay much attention to. Is there any food that may promote intelligence and nourish the brain? Two quite different points of view about the relationship have been proposed for a long time. The theory of "blood-brain strategic pass" explains that every organ gets nutrition through blood circulation except the brain. Because the brain has a strategic pass for selecting, and it is easy for glucose to go through the pass, whatever nutrition you take from food, does not reach the brain. Other nutritionists consider that "it is possible to improve the brain by coordinating the diet, and claim some food can promote intelligence," especially in children.

The nutritionists of the world got an affirmative answer after nearly 20 years' research. Research Dr. Setsuo Iino, a Japanese professor in the Dyida University, and USSR scholars corrected the "blood-brain strategic pass" theory in the early 1980s. They pointed out that "it is a misunderstanding in the cerebral physiology," which affirms the function of food in promoting intelligence and nourishing the brain. It has been proved that thought, memory and quickness in movement bear a close relation to the food taken every day. So continued taking of food for promoting intelligence is good for the brain.

China has a long history of promoting intelligence with food. In the past 20 years, there have been more and more reports about this topic. Much attention has been paid to promoting intelligence of infants and teenagers. It is well known that the development of the brain is closely related to the general nutrimental condition of a person in certain periods of growth. Take the intelligence level of a 17-year-old person as 100 percent, that of a four-year-old one would be 50 percent and an 8-year-old 80 percent. So the period from the last three months of the pregnancy to eight-year-old is most important for the development of the brain. For promoting intelligence with food, the earlier the better.

As early as 2,000 years ago, the earliest classical book on Chinese materia medica, *Shen Nong's Materia Medica,* recorded 49 kinds of herbs having the function of "making clever," "promoting intelligence," "never forgetful" "tonifying the brain" and "reinforcing the *qi* of the heart," etc. Among them, 47 percent are food.

Functional food to promote intelligence has been designed according to basis.

The Design Basis:
(1) The theory of TCM covers the relation between mentality and viscera.

The theory of TCM holds that mental ability has a close relation to the brain, and also to the heart, the kidney, the spleen, the stomach, the liver, the gall-bladder and so on.

Heart: According to the theory of TCM, "the heart stores the vessel, the vessel controls the mental faculties." The ancient scholars considered that the brain was in charge of thinking, but it was dependent on the blood of heart. So a deficiency of blood can cause insomnia. Thinking too hard will impair the heart and spleen and lead to poor memory.

Kidney: The kidney is considered to be "the congenital foundation." The kidney stores the essence, which produces marrow. The marrow consists of two parts: spinal marrow and bone marrow. The spinal marrow ascends to connect with the brain, which is formed by a collection of marrow. If the marrow is insufficient, the intelligence will be very low.

Brain: After eating foods, the nutrient elements will enter blood through digestion and absorption. The blood and essence promote each other. They can be turned into marrow. Chapter 33 of *Miraculous Pivot* therefore states, "The brain is a sea of marrow." So, the brain controls memory, thinking, etc.

Spleen and stomach: The brain needs nutrients. Water and food are the main sources of the nutrients required by the body after birth. The function of the spleen is digestion, absorption, and transport of nutrients.

Liver: Liver regulates *qi* and helps digestion.

Promoting intelligence with food that nourishes the brain doesn' t mean only providing brain with nutrition, but, under the guidance of the theory of TCM, having a proper diet based on an overall analysis of symptoms and signs, then attaining the purpose of nourishing the brain, promoting intelligence and treating oligophrenia. What is the food to promote intelligence? At first, we should know the definition of intelligence. Modern psychologists consider that intelligence is about the ability to study, to recall and the ability to adapt, etc. According to the TCM theory of mental activity, the concept of intelligence includes spirit, wisdom, will, aspiration, meditation, etc. I have divided the foods for promoting intelligence recorded in classical materia medica books into six groups, i.e., promoting intelligence, improving memory, strengthening the will, filling marrow and nourishing the brain, benefiting the spirit and nourishing the heart. The foods that fulfill one of these six functions are taken as the foods for promoting intelligence.

About 100 kinds of food for promotion of intelligence have been selected from 40 books on materia medica. For instance, foods which promote intelligence are longan, sesame, Chinese yam, etc. Foods which improve memory are Poria with hostwood, sesame, animal's heart.

The foods with the function of strengthening the will are grape, honey, edible fungus. Foods with the function of filling marrow and nourishing the brain are the fruit of Chinese wolfberry, tuber of fleece-flower root, sea cucumber, pig's marrow. Foods with the function of benefiting the spirit are lotus seed and garlic, etc. The foods with the function of nourishing the heart are lotus root and milk.

(2) Paying more attention to the clinical application.

In order to verify foods with claims of promoting intelligence, more than 20 kinds of medical classics have been consulted for instance, *Essentially Treasured Prescriptions for Emergencies, Imperial Benevolent Prescriptions of the Taiping Period, General Collection for Holy Relief.*

From the recent publications such as *Collection of Medicated Diet, Chinese Medicated Diet, Medicated Diet in Sichuan Province, Medicated Porridge for Prolonging Life* and *Medicated Porridge Therapy,* 117 prescriptions that promote intelligence have been selected. Surprisingly, the foods recorded in the classic books are found useful to be as the foods used in the clinical practice.

(3) Combining the results of modern research.

The nutritionists of the world hold that the elements with the function of promoting intelligence and benefiting the brain are fat, vitamin C, calcium, carbohydrate, protein, vitamins B, A, E, etc. It has been proved by modern research that the food products with the function of benefiting the brain are the same as those from the table of nutrition of the foods that promote intelligence. We can see clearly that the foods that promote intelligence documented in the ancient books of materia medica have the nutrition proved by modern nutritionists.

(4) Drawing on the valuable experience of professors and experts.

For instance, Xie Haizhou, a professor in the Guang An Men hospital, pays more attention to the food therapy of reinforcing the kidney and tonifying the brain, nourishing the heart and promoting intelligence based on the symptoms and signs in treating children suffered from oligophrenia. The foods and herbs used by him are mulberry, black sesame, longan, raisin, yuber of fleece-flower, Poria, day lily, fruit of Chinese wolfberry, Chinese yam, etc.

(5) Arranging diet according to the psychological character of the children in the different periods of their growing.

According to the five principles mentioned above, the foods such as Poria, longan aril, sesame, litchi, Chinese yam, milk, mulberry, lotus roots, fruit of Chinese wolfberry, animal heart, grape, cherry, lily, Chinese date, walnut, tuber of fleece-flower, raisin, soy bean, millet, lotus seeds, honey, dried day lily, carrot, egg, corn, pig's liver, peanuts and fish, especially seafish, are good for the brain. According to my research, there were more than 100 kinds of foods that have the function of promoting intelligence in classical books about materia medica.

There were some other foods that have the same function, but they are not easy to find.

According to the modern research, they are pig's liver, sheep's liver, fish, egg, peanut, bean curd, ginseng, fruit, vegetable, etc.

Besides, Japanese professor, Mr. Setsuo Iino, considers that white sugar and rice are not good for the brain. If a child takes too much of them without any other food, he gets more chance having mental-disorder. So Mr. Setsuo Iino suggests that mothers should offer their baby vegetable, fruits, bean, animal meat, eggs, etc., but not cake, sugar and sweet drinks. There was a famous child called Jin Xiong Rong in Korea. His mother said that his main food was vegetable and fruit. He was the cleverest child in the world at that time. His IQ (Intelligence Quotient) was 210, the highest level. At 100 days after his birth, he could speak a simple sentence, at five months, he could remember the names of plants, at eight months, he began to study, at three to four years old, and he could speak English and German. However, a suitable amount of meat is necessary.

Common Chinese Functional Food
for Promoting Intelligence

Invigorate the Brain Porridge

Process: Wash 100g rice, put in a pot. Add 25g walnut, 10g dried lily and 20g black sesame. Add water, cook it over a low heat, bring to boil until well done and serve.

Preserved Fruit for Promoting Intelligence

Process: Wash 50g longan aril and 50g Chinese date. 50g litchis, 50g dried grape, and put them into a pot. Add water; cook it over a low heat. When tender add 200g honey.

Chinese Yam and Cuttlefish Rolls

Process: Remove gills and viscera of 500g cuttlefish, clean and cut in half lengthwise, then with cut surface up, cut 1cm square slices. Wash Chinese yam and cut into strips. Pour the peanut oil in a pot and set the pot over a high heat. When the oil begins to smoke drop in the ginger, scallions, garlic and the cuttlefish slices. When they start to curl add the Chinese yam strips, add salt, gourmet powder, yellow wine to taste. Mix with a little starch and pour a little sesame oil over it. Before eating you can put some pepper on it.

Poria and Variegated Carp

Process: Clean a variegated carp (about 1,000g). Take out the meat, chop it finely with the back of a knife. Cut the head off. Set aside. Place the fish meat in a bowl, add 20g powder of Poria, 5g starch, salt, gourmet powder, scallions, ginger, yellow rice wine to taste and mix. Stir well. Add enough water to cover the fish in a pot, bring to boil and put little balls of the fish meat into the water. Simmer over a low heat. When it is almost done, add a little salt, gourmet powder and bamboo shoot. When the head of fish is done, serve.

6.1.4 Building up Strength

"Building up strength" means promoting physical strength. There were some other sayings in Chinese classical literature. For instance, "strong physical strength," "with redoubled physical strength," "good for physical strength," "not easily tired," "good at walking," etc. In daily life, it is very important to build up strength with food and functional food, in order to meet the need of physical labor and training. In recent years, some scientists in the world have searched for foods which are good for people involved in physical activities such as sportsmen and sportswomen, soldiers and astronauts. But what foods can be used to build up strength, provide energy for an explosive effort or recover physical strength? The theory of TCM holds that the most important thing is to build up a strong constitution, and balance the function of *yin, yang, qi* and blood.

From the viewpoint of the differentiation of symptoms and sign used by TCM, there are many causes of tiredness. For instance, exhaustion with difficulty to breath and palpitation are due to deficiency of *qi*. The principle of treatment is to invigorate *qi*. Exhaustion with blurring of vision and dizziness are due to insufficiency of blood. So the principle of treatment is to invigorate blood. Exhaustion with thirst is due to insufficiency of *yin*. So the principle of treatment is to reinforce the body fluid and nourish the blood.

In addition, the food taken before work is different from the food taken after work. Generally speaking, the food with the function of benefiting *qi* and strengthening *yang* are good for before work; while the food for nourishing blood and reinforcing *yin* are good for after work.

Herba Agrimoniae and Chinese Date Honey Syrups

Process: Wash 200g Herba Agrimoniae, 400g Chinese dates, soak fully with water and simmer. Every 20 minutes, collect the infusion, add more water and continue to cook. Remove the collections, and combine them and continue to cook over low heat, until very thick. Add 300g honey. Bring to boil, cool, and store in a jar. Mix one tablespoonful with boiling water, and drink. This can be taken instead of tea.

Ginseng and Quail Eggs

Process: Put 10g ginseng in a pot, soak with cold water for 4 hours. Add 1,000g chicken soup and 20 quail eggs that have been peeled. Simmer for one hour. Place the quail in a plate. Mix starch, sugar, salt, gourmet powder to taste and then cook over heat until it becomes a clear and thick soup, pour over the quail eggs on the plate.

Quick-Fried Mutton Slices with Scallions, Epemedium and Curculigo Rhizome

Process: Wash 10g Herba Epimedii, 10g Rhizoma Curculiginis. Put them in a pot, add some water, and cook over a low heat for 45 minutes. Cut 250g mutton into strips. Cut 50g green Chinese onion into strips too.

Pour the medical herbs soup into a bowl; add starch and mutton strips, mix well. When oil becomes hot enough, add the mutton strips, green Chinese onion, soy sauce, sugar, vinegar, yellow wine and gourmet powder to taste. When the mutton strips are tender remove from the heat and serve.

Black Bone Chicken and Mulberry

Process: Pluck and eviscerate one black bone chicken and clean it. Place in a pot, add dried mulberry (about 50g) and water. Cook over a low heat until tender, add bamboo shoots and cucumbers, salt, gourmet powder, yellow wine to taste, continue to cook until tender.

Chinese Yam, Rhizoma Polygonati and Bean Curd Thick Soup

Process: Cut 100g bean curd and 100g chicken blood into strips. Soak 10g Rhizoma Polygonati in the cold water. Cut 50g Chinese yam into strips. Put in a pot and add some chicken soup. Cook it over heat until tender; add salt, yellow wine, gourmet powder to taste. Add little bamboo shoots and cucumbers. When it is done, mix with a little starch and serve.

6.1.5 Improving Vision

There was an old saying, "The eyes are the windows of the soul." Everybody wants to have good eyesight. It is very important to improve vision with foods in our daily life.

The theory of TCM considers that the liver has its specific body opening in the eyes. Its meridian directly connects with the eyes. Liver blood and *yin* invigorate the eyes. Therefore, insufficiency and excessiveness of the liver will influence the eyes. For instance, insufficiency of liver-*yin* can cause dryness of the eyes. Over sufficiency of liver blood can cause blurring of vision and dizziness; flaming-up of liver-heat can cause redness of the eyes and pain in the eyes, sthenia of liver-*yang* can cause blurring of vision and headache, etc. So the principle of treatment should be reinforcing the liver and kidney-*yin*, nourishing the heart and liver blood, calming the liver to reduce the abnormal rise liver-*yang*, and reduce liver-heat.

Common Medicated Food for Improving Vision

Pale Butterflybush Flower (flos Buddlejae) and Mutton Liver

Process: Clean 1,000g mutton liver and put into a pot together with 50g Flos Buddlejae. Add some water; cook it over a low heat until tender. Cut the liver into slices before eating. Soy sauce, vinegar, etc., are applicable.

Chrysanthemum Flowers and Cassia Drink

Process: Fry 5g Semen Cassiae over low heat until they become yellow. Put them together with 5g dried chrysanthemum flowers in a cup and pour boiling water in it. Cover, and stew for half an hour. Drink it often, several times a day instead of tea.

Roast Wild Chicken with Wemen Celosiae

Process: Pluck and eviscerate one wild chicken (about 1,000g) and clean it. Place it in a pot, add 30g Semen Celosiae (wrap them in cloth). Cook it over low heat until half done; add soy sauce, salt, sugar, yellow wine and gourmet powder to taste. When it becomes tender, remove from the pot, and fry deeply until it becomes yellow and serve. It can be taken as cold dish.

6.1.6 Clear Hearing

"Clear hearing" is to strengthen and improve the ability to hear. Since ancient times, everybody would like to have a "good ear" and there was a Chinese folktale about a person who could hear voices from far away.

The theory of TCM holds that the kidney is an opening into the ear. The liver's meridian communicates the two ears. So the ability of hearing has a close relationship with the kidney and liver.

The common hearing fault is deafness (mild and serious). The causes are insufficiency of the kidney-*yin* and *qi*. In contrast, the cause of tinnitus is insufficiency of liver-*yin* and flaming up of excessive heat of the liver or exuberance of liver-*yang*.

Common Functional Food in TCM Food for Clear Hearing

Fried Pork Kidney with the Root
of Kudzu Vine's Powder and Dogwood Fruit

Process: Soak dogwood fruit in yellow wine for 10 days. Clean 200g pig's kidney and remove sinews, membranes and glands, then cut into pretty shapes. Mix with some starch and then stir-fry quickly in hot vegetable oil, until tender. Flavor with soy sauce, scallions, and ginger. Pour the dogwood fruit wine, and then add the root of Kudzu vine's powder.

Preserved Fruit of Plum for Clear
Liver and Clear Hearing

Process: Put 10g leaves of bluish dogbane in a pot, add some water and cook for 20 minutes. Collect the liquid. Soak 1,000g plum in boiling water. Remove the peels and pips. Place plum in a pot. Add the leaves of bluish dogbane liquid. When all liquids have been absorbed, add honey to taste, and continue to cook and stir until dry.

Boiled Sword Bean and Root of Celery

Process: Soak 100g dried sword bean in the warm water. Cut 200g of the root of celery into strips. Place the sword bean in a pot, add chicken soup, cook it over a heat until half cooked, add the root of celery, salt, gourmet powder to taste, continue to cook until tender, absorb the liquid and serve.

6.1.7 Improving One's Dental Health

The theory of TCM holds that the teeth are the door and window of *zang-fu*. So the teeth can show the insufficiency or excessiveness of *yin, yang, qi* and blood.

The teeth are closely related to the kidney, stomach, and large intestine. According to TCM theory, the meridian of large intestine connects with the upper gums and the meridian of stomach connects with the lower gums.

Therefore, the causes of trouble with teeth are insufficiency of the kidney-*yin*, a flaring up of the asthenia fire caused by deficiency of vital essence of the kidney, deficiency of the stomach-*yin*, dampness and heat accumulated in the stomach and spleen, accumulation of heat in the large intestine, etc. So the approach to improving good dental health is to reinforce the kidney and keeping fire going downward, nourishing the stomach and clearing away heat, removing dampness, etc.

Common Functional Food for Maintaining Dental Health

Dendrobium and Green Tea Drink

Process: Cut 4g dendrobium into pieces. Put green tea and dendrobium in a cup and soak in boiling water. Drink often instead of tea. The tea can be taken after a meal as the water of clean teeth.

Portulacae and Bone Marrow Porridge

Process: Wash 100g rice, and put into a pot, add 15g portulacae that has been cut into pieces and pork bone marrow soup; cook over low heat until it becomes porridge, add salt, gourmet powder, sesame oil and serve.

Fried Freshwater Mussel with Wosun Lettuce

Process: Clean 200g freshwater mussels. First remove and discard the root end and leaves of the wosun and peel the stem. Wash it under the cold running water and cut into strips. Pour a little peanut oil in a pot. When the oil is hot, put the freshwater mussels in, while they are cooking add wosun lettuce. Mix salt, sugar, ginger, scallions, gourmet powder and yellow wine to taste. When it is done, mix with starch and pour a little sesame oil over it.

"Eight-Treasures" Duck for Reinforcing the Kidney and Improving Dental Health

Process: Pluck and eviscerate one white duck, clean and put the black sesame, walnut, mulberry (20g each); lotus seeds, semen euryales, Chinese date, semen coicis that have been soaked in water (20g each) and glutinous rice in the duck, sew up with thread. Then place the duck in a big bowl. Add salt, yellow wine, gourmet powder to taste and some water. Then steam it until it is cooked. Remove stitches before eating.

6.1.8 Beautifying the Hair

Beautifying the hair, including "pitch-black beard," "black hair," "regrowing-hair," and "beautifying the beard" in ancient China.

There was an old saying in China, "Control the whole body by holding a hair." The theory of TCM considered that a hair is very thin and small but it is related closely to *zang-fu*. The hair can reflect the preponderance or discomfiture of *qi*, blood, and *yin* and *yang* of *zang-fu*.

According to the theory of TCM, essence and blood promote each other. When the essence is sufficient, then blood will flourish. Nourishment of the hair requires a sufficient supply of blood, while the vitality of the hair is rooted in the kidney-*qi*. The hair, therefore, shows both a surplus of blood on the one hand, and is an outward manifestation of the kidney on the other. Growth or loss of luster or withering of the hair are all related to the condition of the kidney-*qi*. During the childhood, the kidney-*qi* is in a flourishing state and the hair is lustrous; at old age the kidney-*qi* declines and the hair turns white and falls out. Chapter 10 of *Plain Questions* states: "The kidney dominates bone and is evident in the hair."

In short, the hair includes the hair on the head, eyebrow, eyelash, beard, etc. Ailments are due to the imbalance of the heart, spleen, liver and kidney's function, and family inheritance, disease and physical and chemical factors, i.e., radiotherapy and chemotherapy.

If a teenager's hair becomes thick and white, it is due to blood heat. It is often accompanied by a reddened tongue, thirst, mental irritability, seminal emission, advanced menstruation, the sensation of heat felt in the palm and soles, etc.

So the principle of beautifying the hair is to reinforce the kidney, fill the marrow, regulate the liver and nourish blood, reinforce *yin*, and clear away the heat, etc.

Common Food and Herbal Medicines for Beautifying the Hair

Broad bean, black soy bean, red bean, honey, Chinese date, longan, fruit of Chinese wolfberry, mulberry, sea cucumber and abalone, carrot, tuber of fleece-flower are the common food for beautifying the hair.

Syrup to Darken the Hair

Process: Soak and reconstitute the following: 200g knotted tuber, 200g Poria, 50g angelica, 50g fructus lycii, 50g semen cuscutae, 50g Radix Achyranthis Bidentate, 50g fructus psoraleae, and 50g black sesame seeds. Place in a pot and cook. Every 20 minutes collect the liquid, add some more water, and continue cooking. Take 3 collections. Combine the collections, and cook over high heat, then simmer over low heat until thick and syrupy. Add twice as much honey as liquid in the pot, mix well, and bring to a boil. Remove from heat, cool, and store in a jar.

6. 2 For Supplementary Treatment

6.2.1 Common Cold of Wind-Cold Type

Manifestations: Strong aversion to cold, slight fever without sweating, headache, stuffy nose, watery nasal discharge, itch of the throat, cough, expectoration of thin white sputum, absence of thirst or thirst and desire for a hot drink, aching pain of limbs, thin and white fur, floating pulse or floating and tense pulse.

Sweet Ginger Drink

Ingredients: Fresh ginger 10g
Brown sugar 15g

Process: Wash the fresh ginger, cut into shreds, and place in porcelain mug. Pour on boiling water and leave, covered for 5 minutes. Add brown sugar. Be careful not to add too much.

Usage: Take as warm as possible. For the best result, the patient should sleep after drinking, with his body well covered in order to sweat.

Indications: Wind-cold manifested by fever, headache, body aches, and lack of sweat, poor appetite and nausea.

Source: *Folk Effective Recipes*

Sweet Ginger and Perilla Drink

Ingredients: Fresh ginger 3g
Perilla leaves 3g
Brown sugar 15g

Process: Wash the fresh ginger and perilla leaves, and cut into fine shreds. Place in a cup, then add brown sugar. Pour in boiling water and cover, steeping for 10 minutes.

Usage: Drink while warm.

Indications: Headache and fever, and other symptoms of cold due to wind-cold. nausea, stomach pain and bloating due to stomach-cold, and above symptoms that occur due to poisoning from eating fish and shrimp.

Source: *Collection of Herbalism*

Fermented Bean, Scallions, and Rice Wine Soup

Ingredients: Fermented bean 50g
　　　　　　Scallion leaves 30g
　　　　　　Rice wine 50ml

Process: Add a small bowl of water to the fermented beans and cook for 10 minutes. Add washed scallion leaves, and continue cooking 5 minutes, finally, add rice wine.

Usage: Take while hot.

Indications: Cold, fever, headache, agitation, and lack of sweat as well as nausea, abdominal pain, and diarrhea.

Source: *Meng Shen's Prescriptions*

6.2.2　Common Cold of Wind-Heat Type

Manifestations: Higher fever, slight aversion to wind, slow sweat, distending pain in the head, stuffy nose, yellow and turbid nasal discharge, red-swollen and sore throat, or dry mouth and throat, thirst and strong desire for drink, cough, sticky or yellow phlegm, red margin at tip of the tongue with thin and white fur or light yellowish fur, floating and rapid pulse.

Mulberry, Chrysanthemum, Mint and Bamboo Drink

Ingredients: Mulberry leaves 5g
　　　　　　Chrysanthemum flower 5g
　　　　　　Bitter bamboo leaves 30g
　　　　　　Woolly grass rhizome 30g
　　　　　　Mint 3g

Process: In a teapot place the clean mulberry leaves and chrysanthemum blossoms. Add the bitter bamboo leaves, woolly grass rhizome, and mint. Pour in boiling water and steep for 10 minutes.

Usage: This can be taken in large quantities when cooled.

Indications: Wind-heat manifested by fever, headaches, blurred vision, sore throat and acute conjunctivitis.

Source: *Effective Recipes of Cold Tea in Guangdong Province*

Tea of Chrysanthemum Flower and Reed Rhizome
Ingredients: Chrysanthemum flower 6g
　　　　　　　Reed rhizome 21g (double it if it is used fresh)
Process: Decoct them or infuse them in boiling water.
Usage: To be taken as a drink.
Indications: Common cold of wind-heat type.
Source: *Chinese Medicated Diet*

Drink of Mulberry Leaf, Chrysanthemum Flower, Peppermint and Prepared Soybean
Ingredients: Mulberry leaf 9g
　　　　　　　Chrysanthemum flower 9g
　　　　　　　Peppermint 6g
　　　　　　　Fermented soybean 6g
　　　　　　　Reed rhizome 15g (double the amount if fresh)
Process: Decoct them in water or infuse them for drinking instead of tea.
Usage: The decoction is to be taken several times each day.
Indications: Common cold of wind-heat type.
Source: *Chinese Medicated Diet*

6.2.3 Common Cold of Summer-Heat and Dampness Type
Manifestations: Common cold complicated with summer-heat and dampness syndromes, such as nausea, vomiting, diarrhea and thirst, etc.

Porridge of Job's Tears Seed and Hyacinth Bean
Ingredients: Job's tears seed 30g
　　　　　　　White hyacinth bean 30g
　　　　　　　Rice 100g
Process: Make porridge with the three ingredients.
Usage: To be taken twice a day.
Indications: Applicable to patients with common cold of summer-heat and dampness type.
Source: *100 Cases of Drink Therapy*

Wrinkled Giant-Hyssop Drink
Ingredients: Fresh leaves of wrinkled giant-hyssop 12g (6g if dried leaves are used)
　　　　　　　Fresh lotus leaf 12g (6g if dried)

Sugar in right amount

Process: Decoct them in water or infuse them in boiling water.

Usage: To be taken as a drink.

Indications: It is applicable to those suffering from common cold of summer-heat and dampness type.

Source: *Chinese Medicated Diet*

Watermelon and Tomato Juice

Ingredients: Watermelon 1,000g

　　　　　　Tomato 500g

Process: Remove the flesh of the watermelon, pick out the seeds and squeeze through cheesecloth. Mix the two kinds of juice together.

Usage: Use in place of drinking water.

Indications: Summer-cold, fever, thirst, agitation, poor appetite, indigestion, and burning urination.

Source: *Folk Effective Recipes*

Cough

A cough is the main symptom for lung problems and may result either from an attack by exogenous pathogenic factors disturbing the dispersion of *qi* of the lung, or from disorders of the lung itself or other diseased *zang-fu* organs affecting the lung.

6.2.4　Cough Due to Wind-Cold

Manifestations: Cough with itching of throat, thin and white expectoration, often accompanied with aversion to cold, fever without sweating, stuffy nose, watery nasal discharge, headache, aching pain in the limbs and so on, thin and whitish fur, floating or floating and tense pulse.

Ginger and Fermented Soy Bean Malt Candy

Ingredients: Dried ginger 30g

　　　　　　Fermented soy beans 15g

　　　　　　Malt sugar 250g

Process: Place the dried ginger and fermented soy beans in a pot, add water to cover, and boil and simmer. Every 30 minutes, remove the liquid and save. Add more water and continue to cook. Collect liquid twice, combine, and boil down. When thick, add the malt sugar and mix well.

Cook until threads form when dripped and remove from heat. Mix and knead until the candy turns a milky white color, then turn out on a greased plate. Cool, and cut into about 100 pieces.

Usage: To be taken as desired.

Indications: This will warm the lungs and aid digestion. It will alleviate the cough of bronchitis caused by infection or coldness in the lungs, as well as white sticky phlegm, fever, congestion and agitation.

Source: *A Supplement to Handbook of Prescriptions for Emergencies*

Honeyed Radish

Ingredients: Honey 30g
    White radish, one piece
    Dried ginger 3g
    Ephedra 3g

Process: Place all the ingredients in a bowl and steam them. When they are done, discharge the ginger and the ephedra, and keep the honey and radish for eating.

Usage: To be taken as desired.

Indications: It is applicable to acute bronchitis of wind-cold type.

Source: *Prescriptions for Caring All People*

Porridge of Perilla Leaves and Apricot Kernel

Ingredients: Perilla leaves 9g
    Bitter apricot kernel 9g
    Tangerine peel 6g
    Rice 50g

Process: Decoct three ingredients in water first, sift the liquid from the dregs, then put the rice in with the right amount of water and make them into a porridge.

Usage: Eat twice daily.

Indications: It is applicable to acute bronchitis of wind-cold type.

Source: *Chinese Medicated Diet*

6.2.5   Cough Due to Wind-Heat

Manifestations: Cough, dry and painful throat, difficult expectoration, ropy phlegm or thick and yellow phlegm, often accompanied with symptoms of aversion to wind, fever, thirst perspiration, yellow nasal discharge, headache and so on, thin and yellow fur, floating and rapid pulse or floating and slippery pulse.

Towel Gourd Flowers and Honey Drink
Ingredients: Fresh towel gourd flower 10g
Honey, a little
Process: Clean the fresh towel gourd flowers and steep in hot water in a porcelain cup for 10 minutes.
Usage: Add honey to taste, and drink very hot 3 times a day.
Indications: Acute and chronic bronchitis due to lung-heat, coughing of yellow sputum, asthma, chest pains, and dry mouth.
Source: *Herbalism in Yunnan Province*

Pear Honey
Ingredients: Pear 1,500g
Fresh ginger 250g
Process: Wash the pears. Remove the seeds, and cut into small pieces. Squeeze the juice out through a clean cloth. Wash the fresh ginger, cut into thin strips and squeeze the juice out through a cloth. Place the pear juice in a pot, and cook over high heat. Reduce heat, and continue to simmer until thick and syrupy. Add twice as much honey as liquid in the pot. Add the ginger juice, and bring the mixture to a boil. Remove from heat, cool, and store in a jar.
Usage: Dissolve one tablespoonful of pear honey in boiling water. Drank several times a day instead of tea.
Indications: Coughing, yellow phlegm, and sore throat due to lung-heat.
Source: *Probing the Origin of Herbalism*

Drink of Chrysanthemum Flower and Apricot Kernel
Ingredients: Chrysanthemum flowers 6g
Bitter apricot kernel 6g
Mulberry leaves 6g
Liquorice 3g
Process: Infuse all the ingredients in boiling water.
Usage: To be taken as a drink.
Indications: It is suitable for acute bronchitis of wind-heat type.
Source: *Chinese Medicated Diet*

6.2.6 Cough Due to Deficiency or Dryness of the Lung

Manifestations: Frequent cough, shortness of breath, low voice, pale complexion, lassitude, pale tongue with thin and white fur, and thready and weak pulse attributed to deficiency of the lung-*qi*; symptoms of frequent dry cough or cough with little or blood-tinged sputum, night sweat, dry mouth and throat, feverish sensation in the palms and soles, or low fever, red tongue with thin fur, and thready and rapid pulse caused by deficiency of the lung-*yin*.

Ginger Syrup

Ingredients: Ginger juice 200g
Honey 200g
Process: Bring the ginger juice and the honey together to the boil in a pot. Cook until very syrupy. Cool and store in a jar.
Usage: Take 30ml dissolved in boiled water twice daily.
Indications: This will cure prolonged cough due to coldness or dryness in the lung.
Source: *Essentially Treasured Prescriptions for Emergencies*

Lard Syrup

Ingredients: Lard 100g
Honey 100g
Process: Separately bring the lard and the honey to the boil over a low flame. Remove from heat, and cool to lukewarm. Mix the lard and honey together.
Usage: Eat one tablespoon directly, twice daily.
Indications: This strengthens and moistens dryness and will cure dry lung and coughing, dry intestines and constipation, and physical emaciation.
Source: *Compendium of Materia Medica*

Malt Sugar and Soy Bean Milk

Ingredients: Malt sugar 20g
Soy bean milk 250ml
Process: Put one tablespoon of malt sugar in a bowl, and pour in vigorously boiling soy bean milk.
Usage: Mix thoroughly, and drink.
Indications: This will strengthen and nourish the *yin*. It is good for debility and prolonged dry cough.

6.2.7 Cough Due to Sputum and Dampness

Manifestations: Cough, white and abundant phlegm which is ropy and greasy or thick, oppressed feeling in the chest and epigastric region, poor appetite, lassitude, white and greasy fur, soft and floating and slippery pulse.

Honeyed Pomelo

Ingredients: Fresh pomelo 500g
    Honey 250g
    Wine, a little

Process: Remove the seed from the fresh pomelo, cut into pieces, and place in a jar. Add some wine, and seal the jar tightly. Soak overnight. Pour the jar contents into a pot, and boil until the liquids have dried up. Add the honey, and mix thoroughly. Cool, then store in a jar until use.

Usage: To be taken as desired.

Indications: Eaten often, it will cure coughing due to excessive phlegm.

Source: *Compendium of Materia Medica*

Sugared Oranges

Ingredients: Orange 500g
    Sugar 250g

Process: Remove the seeds and peel from the oranges. Put in a pot, add the sugar, and marinate for one day. When the oranges have been saturated with sugar, cook over low heat until all liquids have evaporated, cool, and then use a spoon to flatten and press each orange section. Mix flattened sections with white sugar, then air-dry on a plate for several days. Store in a jar until needed.

Usage: To be taken as desired.

Indications: This will expand the middle and allow flow of *qi*, soothe coughing, and dissolve phlegm. Eaten often, it will cure bloating after meals, and coughing of excessive sputum.

Source: *A Supplement to the Great Herbalism*

Five Flavored Syrup

Ingredients: Pears 1,000g
    White radish 1,000g
    Fresh ginger 250g

Condensed milk 250g

Honey 250g

Rice wine, a little

Process: Remove the seeds from the pears, and cut into pieces. Also cut the white radish and fresh ginger into small pieces. Separately, squeeze the juice out of each item through clean cloth. Combine the pear juice and radish juice in a pot, and cook over high heat, then simmer over low heat, reduce until thick and syrupy. Add the ginger juice. Also add the condensed milk and the honey. Mix evenly, and bring to the boil. Remove from heat, and cool, then store in a jar.

Usage: For each use, dissolve one tablespoon into boiling water, or add a little rice wine. Drink twice daily.

Indications: Fatigue, chills due to pulmonary tuberculosis, and prolonged coughing.

Source: *Collection of Experience and Prescriptions*

6.2.8 Asthma

Asthma is a common illness characterized by repeated attacks of paroxysmal dyspnea with wheezing. Generally speaking, it involves a variety of disorders resulting from disturbance of *qi* activities, and can be divided into two types: deficiency (in most cases as deficiency of the lung, spleen and kidney) and excess (at the stage of attack, there are two types of syndromes, namely, asthma of the cold type and asthma of the heat type).

Eggs and Soy Bean Milk

Ingredients: Egg, one

Soy bean milk 250ml

Sugar, a little

Process: Beat one chicken egg in a large bowl and then pour in soy bean milk that has been brought to the boil. Flavor with sugar to taste.

Usage: To be taken as a drink.

Indications: This will strengthen the body and calm coughing. It is good for physical debility, asthma of a deficiency type, and prolonged coughing.

Source: *A Supplement to the Great Herbalism*

Egg and Turnip Radish

Ingredients: Radish, one

152

Egg, one

Process: Around the winter solstice, select one large turnip radish (reddish-pink skin and white flesh). Cut it down in the middle with a knife, and then scoop out a depression in each of the two halves. Place a whole raw egg in one half with the large end pointing towards the top of the turnip. Replace the other half over the egg, and tie together with string (be careful not to break the egg). Plant the turnip in a plant pot, water well, and keep warm, giving it lot of sunshine, thus keeping the root alive and able to sprout new leaves. After Nine Periods have passed (about 81 days) dig out the turnip, clean off the dirt, and cut open. Remove the egg, and slice the turnip. Put in a pot with some water and boil until done, then crack the egg into the soup (the egg yolk and white will be mixed but not rotten). Do not add any salt. (In order to ensure at least one live turnip, many can be planted at a time. Extra consumption will do no harm.)

Usage: To be taken as soup, one or twice a day.

Indications: Asthma due to allergy.

Source: *Folk Effective Recipes*

Honey-Preserved Lily

Ingredients: Dried lily 100g

Honey 150g

Process: Wash the dried lily and put in a large bowl with the honey. Steam in a steamer for one hour. Mix well while still hot. Cool, and store in a jar until use.

Usage: Eat twice daily.

Indications: This will moisten the lung and stop coughing and asthma, soothe the heart and calm the nerves. It will cure consumptive cough, thick sputum, deficiency in heat, asthma in deficiency type, and agitation.

Source: *Imperial Benevolent Prescriptions of the Taiping Period*

6.2.9 Dizziness

Manifestations: A mild case can be relieved by closing one's eyes, while a serious case has the illusion of bodily movement with a rotary sensation like sitting in a sailing boat or moving car, and even accompanied by nausea, vomiting and sweating. Dizziness can be divided into three types: 1) hyperactivity of the liver-*yang*; 2) deficiency of *qi* and blood; and 3) interior retention of phlegm dampness.

Chrysanthemum and Pagoda Tree Flower and Green Tea Drink

Ingredients: Chrysanthemum flowers 3g
Green tea 3g
Pagoda tree flowers 3g

Process: Wash the chrysanthemum flowers, green tea, and pagoda tree flowers. Place in a porcelain cup, and pour in boiling water. Cover tightly and steep for 5 minutes.

Usage: Drink often, several times a day.

Indications: High blood pressure.

Source: *Folk Effective Recipes*

Chrysanthemum, Hawthorn Fruit and Cassia Drink

Ingredients: Chrysanthemum flowers 3g
Sliced hawthorn fruit 15g
Cassia 15g

Process: Wash the chrysanthemum flowers, and sliced hawthorn fruit, and cassia. Place in a thermos, and pour in boiling water. Cover, and steep for half an hour.

Usage: Drink often, several times a day.

Indications: Hypertension accompanied by coronary artery disease.

Source: *Folk Effective Recipes*

Chrysanthemum Dregs

Ingredients: Chrysanthemum flowers 10g
Fermented glutinous rice, desired amount

Process: Cut the chrysanthemum flowers into pieces. Mix with any amount of fermented glutinous rice and heat.

Usage: Eat twice daily.

Indications: Hypertension and dizziness due to liver-heat.

Source: *Xu Sibo' s Prescriptions*

6.2.10 Palpitation

Palpitation refers to unduly rapid action of the heart which is felt by the patient and accompanied by nervousness and restlessness.

Mild palpitation is mostly due to a sudden fright and overstrain. The general condition is comparatively good and the symptoms are of short duration. A serious case is often due to prolonged internal injury. The general condition is comparatively poor and the symptoms are severe.

Rhizoma Polygonati Odorati Instant

Ingredients: Rhizoma Polygonati Odorati 250g

Sugar 300g

Process: Wash the Rhizoma Polygonati Odorati, and reconstitute in cold water. Simmer in water. Every 20 minutes, collect all the liquid, add some water, and continue cooking. Collect the liquid three times and combine them. Continue to cook the combined infusions and reduce until concentrated and thick, and almost dry. Remove from heat, and cool to warm. Mix in the sugar, dry in the sun, break into pieces, and store in a jar.

Usage: For each use, dissolve 10g in boiling water. Drink three times daily.

Indications: Rheumatic heart disease, pulmons-cardiae disease, and beat failure due to cardiovascular disease.

Source: *Collection of Chinese Materia Medica*

Radix Codonopsis Pilosulae and
Radix Astragali Seu Hedysari Crystals

Ingredients: Radix Codonopsis Pilosulae 250g

Radix Astragali Seu Hedysari 250g

Sugar 500g

Process: Reconstitute Radix Codonopsis Pilosulae and Radix Astragali Seu Hedysari in cold water. Put into water and simmer. Collect the liquid every half an hour, and add some more water, and continue cooking. Collect the liquid three times and combine them. Continue cooking the collections over low heat, and reduce until thick and syrupy. Remove from heat, and mix in the sugar to absorb all the liquids, dry in the sun, and break into pieces and store in a jar.

Usage: For each use, dissolve 10g in boiling water. Drink twice daily.

Indications: Heat palpitations and shortness of breath due to deficiency of *qi*, poor appetite and semi-liquid stool, prolapsed organs, edema, asthma, and dizziness.

Source: *Folk Effective Recipes*

Pig' s Heart in Black Bean Sauce

Ingredients: Pig' s heart 1,000g

Scallions, a little
Ginger, a little
Fermented black beans, a little
Soy sauce, a little
Rice wine, a little

Process: Clean the pig' s heart, and place in a pot. Add scallions, ginger, fermented black beans, soy sauce, and rice wine to taste. Add water and cook over a low heat until the hearts are tender. Remove the heart and cut into thin slices, and place on a flat plate.

Usage: This can be eaten as cold appetizer.

Indications: This dish will fortify the heart and soothe the spirit, and is good for debility of the heart and blood, heart palpitations, and convulsions and palpitations due to fear after labor.

Source: *Reflections of Food Doctors*

6.2.11 Poor Appetite

Poor appetite is a common syndrome of digestive system. The causes of it are retention of food, attack of liver-*qi* to the stomach, deficiency of the spleen-*yang* and stomach-*yang* and so on.

Orange and Date Drink

Ingredients: Chinese jujube, 10 pieces
Fresh orange peel 10g (or 3g dried orange peel)

Process: In a pot scorch 10 large Chinese jujubes, and place in a thermos with the orange peel. Steep in boiling water for 10 minutes.

Usage: Taken before meals instead of tea.

Indications: It will stimulate the appetite. Taken as tea after meals it will cure indigestion.

Source: *Folk Effective Recipes*

Candied Smoked Plum

Ingredients: Smoked plum 250g
Crystal sugar 250g

Process: Wash the smoked plum, place in a pot and soak in water. After soaking, boil and cook until half done. Take out of the pot and remove the seeds. Dice the plum, then return to the original cooking water, add the crushed crystal sugar. Continue cooking until 70 percent done and the liquids have been absorbed. Cool, then coat with a layer of white sugar. Store in a jar until use.

Usage: To be taken as desired.

Indications: This will stimulate the appetite, stimulate salivation, act as an astringent, calm action of roundworms, and relieve dysentery and abdominal pain due to roundworms.

Source: *Cookbook for Food & Drinks in Daily Life*

Tangerine Candy

Ingredients: Powdered tangerine peel 100g
                Sugar 500g

Process: Put the sugar into a pot and add a little water. Cook until syrupy, then add the finely powdered tangerine peel. Continue to cook until threads form when the syrup is dripped, and remove from heat. Pour into a greased plate, cool and cut into about 100 pieces.

Usage: To be taken as desired.

Indications: This candy will strengthen the spleen, stimulate the appetite, sooth coughing, and dispel phlegm. Taken often, it will alleviate poor appetite, indigestion, and a productive cough.

Source: *Folk Effective Recipes*

6.2.12 Stomachache

Stomachache refers to a pain over the epigastrium, which is usually accompanied by epigastric upset, poor appetite, eructation and nausea. It can be classified into: 1) retention of cold in the stomach; 2) retention of food; 3) attack of liver-*qi* to the stomach; 4) stagnation of heat in the liver and stomach; 5) blood stasis; 6) deficiency of stomach-*yin*; and 7) deficiency of the spleen-*yang* and stomach-*yang*.

Candy to Aid Digestion

Ingredients: Red tea 50g
                Sugar 500g

Process: Boil red tea with water. Every 20 minutes, collect the liquid, add more water, and continue to brew. Collect the liquid four times and combine the liquid. Boil the liquid over small flame until it is very concentrated and add the sugar. Mix well, and continue to cook until the syrups form threads when dripped. Pour into a greased plate and cool. Score into 100 or so strips.

Usage: Take after meals.
Indications: Indigestion, stuffed feeling from over-consumption, and stomachache.
Source: *Folk Effective Recipes*

Ginger, Orange, Potato Juice
Ingredients: Potato 100g
              Ginger 10g
              Orange, one
Process: Clean and dice the potato and ginger. Peel one orange and remove the seeds. Put all ingredients in a clean cloth and squeeze out the juice.
Usage: Take one tablespoon before meals.
Indications: Nausea due to nervous stomach, or loss of appetite.
Source: *Folk Effective Recipes*

Vinegar-Soaked Ginger Drink
Ingredients: Fresh ginger 250g
              Vinegar 500ml
              Brown sugar, a little
Process: Wash and slice fresh ginger, and soak the slices in vinegar for at least one night.
Usage: To use, take three slices of ginger, add brown sugar to taste, pour on boiling water, and let steep for a short while. This can be used in place of tea.
Indications: Poor appetite, nausea and vomiting and stomachache.
Source: *Reflections of Food Doctors*

6.2.13   Abdominal Distention

Abdominal distention is a common complaint in a clinic. Distention and fullness are likely to occur in both the upper and lower abdomen. The stomach is located in the upper abdomen, while the small and large intestines are in the lower. They are responsible for the storage, digestion, and assimilation of food and excretion of the wastes. Once the stomach and intestines lose their functions, abdominal distention and pain, belching, vomiting, etc. will occur.

Honey-Preserved Radish

Ingredients: White radishes 500g

Honey 150g

Process: Wash the fresh white radishes, then dice them. Blanch them in boiling water, shake off excess water, and air dry them for half a day. Put back in the pot, add the honey, and bring to the boil over low flame, mix evenly. Cool and store.

Usage: To be taken as desired.

Indications: This will expand the middle, aid digestion, regulate flow of *qi*, and dissolve phlegm. If used after meals, it will cure indigestion, nausea and upset stomach.

Source: *Prescriptions for Caring All People*

Sugared Lemons

Ingredients: Fresh lemons 500g

Sugar 250g

Process: Remove the peel and seeds from the fresh lemons, cut into pieces, and place in a pot with the sugar. Marinate for one day until the lemon pulp has been saturated with sugar. Cook over low flame until the liquids have dried up, then remove from flame and cool. Mix with some more white sugar, and store in a jar until needed.

Usage: To be taken as desired.

Indications: This product will stimulate salivation, thirst, stimulate appetite, and calm the fetus' movements. Eaten often, it will cure poor appetite, dry mouth and excessive thirst, as well as lack of appetite and nausea during pregnancy.

Source: *A Supplement to the Great Herbalism*

Instant Tea with Ginger

Ingredients: Red tea 200g

Fresh ginger juice 200g

Sugar 500g

Process: Add some water to the red tea, and boil. Every 20 minutes, collect the liquid, add some water again and continue cooking. Collect the liquid three times and combine the liquid. Cook the liquid over low flame, reducing until almost dry. Add the fresh ginger juice. Continue to cook until very thick. Remove from heat, and mix in the sugar under the liquid is totally absorbed. Dry in the sun, then break into pieces and store in a jar.

Usage: For each use, dissolve 10g in boiling water. Drink 3 times daily.
Indications: Intestinal infection, bacterial dysentery, and abdominal pain.
Source: *Folk Effective Recipes*

6.2.14 Diarrhea

Diarrhea refers to abnormal frequency and liquidity of fecal discharges. It is usually due to disorders of the spleen, stomach, large and small intestines. In terms of the manifestations of the disease and the course, it is clinically divided into acute and chronic. The former is mostly caused by indigestion due to excessive eating or improper diet and attack of external cold dampness, leading to dysfunction in transmission of intestinal contents, or caused by invasion of damp heat in summer or autumn; the latter is caused by deficiency of the spleen and stomach, leading to failure in transportation and transformation.

It is essential to distinguish diarrhea and dysentery.

Pomegranate Peel Syrup
Ingredients: Fresh pomegranate peel 1,000g
     Honey 300g
Process: Wash and dice the fresh pomegranate peel, add water, and boil. For every 30 minutes, collect the liquid, add more water, and continue cooking. Collect the liquid twice and combine the liquid. Cook the liquid over low flame until it reduced and concentrated. Add the honey. Bring to a boil, then remove from heat. Cool, then store in a jar.
Usage: Take one tablespoon dissolved in hot water twice daily.
Indications: Diarrhea due to indigestion or diarrhea and abdominal pain due to intestinal infection.
Source: *Folk Effective Recipes*

Cooked Rice and Wheat Flour
Ingredients: Rice flour 250g
     Wheat flour 250g
     Sugar, a little
Process: Dry-fry over a low heat the rice flour and wheat flour. Cool, and set aside.
Usage: Every day, mix some with boiling water and flour with a little sugar, and eat.

Indications: This will cure agitation and heat, excessive thirst, and diarrhea. It will cure agitation due to heat illness, excessive thirst and diarrhea.

Source: *Newly Compiled Materia Medica of the Tang Dynasty*

Lotus Seeds and Pig's Tripe

Ingredients: Pig's tripe, one
Lotus seeds, 40 pieces
Sesame oil, a little
Salt, a little
Scallions, a little
Ginger, a little
Garlic, a little

Process: Clean one pig's tripe. Stuff it with 40 water-soaked lotus seeds, and tie with a string. Place it in a pot, and boil until the pig's tripe is thoroughly cooked. After cooling, cut it into strips and put on a plate with the lotus seeds. Add sesame oil, salt, scallions, ginger, and garlic, and mix well.

Usage: To be taken once a day.

Indications: This will strengthen the spleen and fortify the stomach, and strengthen weakness. Eaten often, it will help alleviate poor appetite, emaciation, diarrhea and dropsy.

Source: *Invention of Medicine*

6.2.15　Constipation

Constipation is a decrease in the frequency of bowel movements accompanied by difficult, prolonged effort in passing dry and hard stools. It is mainly caused by the disturbed transmitting function of the large intestine and also related to the function of the spleen, stomach and kidney. It can be divided into two types: deficiency and excess.

Mulberry Syrup

Ingredients: Fresh mulberry 1,000g (or dried product 500g)
Honey 300g

Process: Wash the fresh mulberries. Add to some water, and simmer. Every 30 minutes, collect the infusion, add water and continue to cook. Remove two collections, and combine them, continue to cook over low heat, reduce water until very thick. Add the honey. Bring to a boil, cool, and store in a jar.

Usage: Twice daily, mix one tablespoon in boiling water, and drink.

Indications: This will nourish and fortify the liver and kidneys, and improve hearing and vision. It will cure insomnia, amnesia, dimmed sight and hearing, thirst, constipation, and premature graying of the hair.

Source: *Dictionary of Chinese Medicine*

Pine Nut Candy

Ingredients: Dried fried pine nuts 250g
                Sugar 500g

Process: Put the sugar in a pot with a little water, and cook over low heat until threads form when dripped, remove from heat and immediately mix in the dry fried pine nuts. Pour out on a greased plate and press flat. Score the candy, and when completely cooled, break into small pieces.

Usage: To be taken as desired.

Indications: This will fortify the lungs and spleen, stop coughing and spitting of blood. Taken often, it will cure the cough in chronic bronchitis in the elderly and constipation.

Source: *Renew Herbalism*

Rice Wine and Mashed Walnut Soup

Ingredients: Walnut meat, 5 pieces
                Sugar 50g
                Rice wine 50ml

Process: Place the walnut meat and the sugar in a bowl, and mash with a rolling pin. Put the mashed walnuts in a pot, add the rice wine, and cook over low flame for 10 minutes.

Usage: Take twice daily.

Indications: Neurosthenia, headache, insomnia, amnesia, prolonged asthma, lumbago, and habitual or genatric constipation.

Source: *Compendium of Materia Medica*

6.2.16 Diabetes

Diabetes is a disease characterized by polydipsia, polyphagia, polyuria, emaciation and turbidness and sweetness of the urine, Clinically, diabetes is classified as that involving upper *jiao*, middle *jiao* and Lower *jiao*, which manifests predominantly polydipsia, polyphagia and polyuria, respectively. This disease belongs to the category of "Xiao Ke" in TCM. Recuperation by proper diet plays a very important role in relieving the above symptoms of the patients. Therefore, dietetic Chinese materia medica and health food are comparatively desirable aids in treating this disease.

Carp Steamed with Tea

Ingredients: Carp 500g
Green tea 10g

Process: Clean and remove the gills from the carp, but keep the scale. Stuff the cavity of the fish with green tea leaves, and place it on a plate. Steam the fish until it is cooked.

Usage: Eat only the meat, with no spice.

Indications: This will strengthen and quench thirst. It is suitable for patients with heat disease, or diabetics who are excessively thirsty and cannot stop drinking.

Source: *Orthodox for Saving Lives*

Bitter Melon Tea

Ingredients: Bitter melon, one piece
Green tea, a little

Process: Take one bitter melon and trim the ends. Hollow out the fruit, remove the flesh, and fill the cavity with green tea leaves. Hang the bitter melon in an airy place. After the bitter melon has dried, wash the outside and wipe it dry. Then cut into small pieces along with the green tea, and mix well.

Usage: For each dose, place 10g of the mixture into a thermos, and steep in boiling hot water for half an hour.

Indications: Taken often, this will cure sunstroke heat, thirst, and lack of urine.

Source: *Chinese Materia Medica in Fujian Province*

Water Spinach and Water Chestnut Soup

Ingredients: Water spinach 250g
Water chestnuts 10 pieces
Crystal sugar, desired amount

Process: Wash and chop the water spinach, peel and wash the water chestnuts. Place both in a pot with some water. Cook for half an hour. Before serving, add crystal sugar to taste, then remove from pot.

Usage: This can be eaten at one sitting or several. Eat the vegetable and water chestnut, and drink the soup.

Indications: Dry mouth, sore throat, agitation, and stuffy feeling in the chest due to heat diseases.

Source: *Folk Effective Recipes*

6.2.17 Urinary Infections

Urinary infections, including pyelonephritis, cystitis and urethritis, is characterized clinically by lumbago, frequency and urgency of micturition, and urodynia. It belongs to "Lin Zheng" (stranguria) in TCM. Clinically it is classified as stranguria of heat-type, stranguria associated with hematuria, stranguria due to disorder of Qi, stranguria due to urinary stone, stranguria associated with chyluria and stranguria induced by overstrain.

Winter Melon Soup

Ingredients: Winter melon flesh, one piece

Process: Remove the seeds from some winter melon flesh. Dry in the sun until half-dry, store until used. For each preparation, boil 30g dried winter melon for half an hour.

Usage: This can be taken any time, drink frequently like tea.

Indications: Thirst in heat diseases, agitation, and edema and inability to urinate.

Source: *Imperial Benevolent Prescriptions of the Taiping Period*

Sugar Cane and Lotus Root Juice

Ingredients: Sugarcane 500g

Lotus root 500g

Process: Clean the sugarcane. Remove the skin, cut into small pieces, and squeeze through a clean cloth. Clean the lotus root, remove the joints, and dice. Soak the lotus root dices in the sugarcane juice for half a day, then squeeze through a clean cloth.

Usage: Divide the resulting liquid into three portions, to be taken in one day.

Indications: This will alleviate urinary infections, frequent micturition and hematuria.

Source: *Folk Effective Recipes*

Six to One Lotus Seed Soup

Ingredients: Lotus seeds 60g

Raw liquorice 10g

Crystal sugar, a little

Process: Remove the pith from the lotus seeds. Add to the raw liquorice root, and add one large bowl of water. Cook over low heat until the lotus seeds are tender and add crystal sugar. (This soup is called six to one because of the ratio of quantities of lotus seeds to liquorice root.)

Usage: To be taken once a day.

Indications: Urinary infections, urgent urination, frequent urination, and agitation and coldness.

Source: *Ren Zhai' s Prescriptions*

6.2.18 Edema

Subcutaneous retention of fluid which leads to puffiness of the head, face, eyelids, limbs, abdomen and even the whole body is called edema. The causative factors are invasion of the body by the exogenous pathogenic wind and water dampness, and internal injury by food or overstrain, which results in disturbance of water circulation and overflow of water. Since the water circulation in the body is related to the regulatory function of the lung-*qi*, transporting function of the spleen-*qi*, activity of the kidney-*qi* and water communication of the three *jiao*, the functional derangement of the lung, spleen, kidney and three *jiao* may lead to edema. Clinically edema is divided into two patterns: *yin* edema and *yang* edema.

Pig' s Liver Mung Bean Porridge

Ingredients: Fresh pig' s liver 100g

Mung beans 50g

Rice 100g

Process: Wash the mung beans and the rice. Add some water, and cook into porridge. When almost done, add the washed, sliced fresh pig' s liver. When the pig' s liver is thoroughly cooked, it is ready.

Usage: To be taken once a day. Do not add any salt.

Indications: Eaten often, it will cure weakness and edema due to malnutrition.

Source: *Compendium of Materia Medica*

Corn Silk Instant

Ingredients: Corn silk 1,000g
               Sugar 500g

Process: Wash the corn silk. Add to some water, and cook for one hour. Remove the sediments, and continue cooking over low heat, reducing until almost dry. Remove from heat, cool, and mix in the sugar. Dry in the sun, break into pieces and store in a jar.

Usage: For each use, dissolve 10g in boiling water. Drink three times daily.

Indications: Edema due to nephritis, and back pain and bloody urine due to kidney stones.

Source: *Folk Effective Recipes*

Chinese Yam Poria Buns

Ingredients: Powdered Chinese yam 100g
               Powdered Poria 100g
               Sugar 300g
               Lard, a little
               Shredded green and red preserved plum, a little
               Flour 200g
               Baking soda, a little

Process: Put the powdered Chinese yam and the powdered Poria, add water, and soak and mix into a paste. Steam for half an hour. Mix with the sugar and some lard, and shredded green and red preserved plum (or fruit) to make a filling. Make a dough of flour, let it ferment, and add some baking soda. Wrap dough over the filling to make buns. Steam the buns until done.

Usage: To be taken once a day.

Indications: This will benefit the spleen and stomach and fortify the *yin* and *qi*. Eaten continuously, it will cure physical debility, deficiency of the spleen and stomach, poor appetite, excessive thirst, frequent urination, seminal emission, and bed-wetting.

Source: *The Literati's Care of Their Parents*

6.2.19 Anemia

Anemia, a collective name for iron-deficiency anemia, macrocytic anemia, hemolytic anemia, a plastic anemia and other secondary anemia, is characterized by pale or sallow and lusterless complexion, pale lips and finger-nails, sleepiness, lassitude, shortness of breath, dizziness, palpitation due to exertion, emaciation and bleeding. It belongs in TCM to deficiency of blood or consumptive disease and sallow complexion of insufficiency type. The common types of syndromes are 1) deficiency of the heart, spleen, *qi* and blood; and 2) deficiency of the liver-*yin*, kidney-*yin*, essence and blood.

Sugar Preserved Chinese Jujube with Additions

Ingredient: Dried Chinese jujube 50g

Peanuts 100g

Brown sugar 50g

Process: Wash the dried Chinese jujubes and reconstitute in warm water. Briefly boil the peanuts, cool, and remove the skins. Place the reconstituted red dates and peanut skin in the peanut-boiling water, add some more cold water, and cook over low flame for about half an hour. Remove the peanut skins, add the brown sugar, and cook until the sugar has dissolved and the liquids have been absorbed.

Usage: To be taken in the ratio of 10 jujubes and 20 peanuts per day.

Indications: This food fortifies *qi* and the blood. It is beneficial for deficiency of blood after disease or giving birth, nutritional and pernicious anemia, platelet deficiency, and abnormal blood situations due to radiation therapy or chemotherapy for cancer.

Source: *Folk Effective Recipes*

Pig's Intestines in Coriander Sauce

Ingredients: Pig's intestines 500g

Fresh coriander 100g

Vegetable oil, a little

Scallions, a little

Ginger, a little

Soy sauce, a little

Salt, a little

Process: Clean the pig's intestines and the fresh coriander. Stuff the intestines with coriander and tie each end with string. Boil in a pot over a low flame until seven-10ths done, then remove intestines, cut open stirring and remove coriander. Cut the intestines into small round slices. In a pot, heat a little vegetable oil and add scallions and ginger. Then add the intestines, soy sauce, table salt, white sugar, and yellow rice wine to taste. Pour in some of the boiling water and coriander and boil. When the liquid has boiled down, add some starch, and cook until clear. Place on a flat plate, and sprinkle on some fresh uncooked coriander.

Usage: To be taken once a day for a week.

Indications: This dish will fortify general weakness, deficiency of blood and cure intestinal bleeding. It is of great help to those with blood in the stool.

Source: *Prescriptions for Emergencies*

Red-Cooked Turtle

Ingredients: Turtle 250-500g
Vegetable oil 30ml
Fresh ginger, a little
Scallions, a little
Black pepper, a little
Sugar, a little
Soy sauce, a little
Rice wine, a little

Process: Select one turtle weighing 250-500g, cut the head off, remove the entrails and cut into pieces. In vegetable oil, fry ginger, scallions, black pepper and sugar together, then add soy sauce and rice wine before putting in the turtle meat. Add water, and simmer until tender.

Usage: To be taken once a day for five days.

Indications: This dish benefits *yin* and fortifies the blood. It will help lower heat, blood in coughing, and blood in the stool.

Source: *Food Therapy for Laymen*

6.2.20   Nose Bleeding

Nose bleeding is a common disease, which can be classified into four types: 1) Attack of the lungs by heat manifested by bleeding from the nose, dryness of nose, throat and mouth or fever, dry cough, red tongue with thin yellow coat and rapid pulse. 2) Hyperactivity of stomach-heat manifested by bleeding of fresh blood from the nose, dryness of nose and mouth, halitosis, irritability, constipation, swelling and pain of gingiva or bleeding from gum, red tongue with yellow coating and rapid pulse. 3) Hyperactivity of liver-fire manifested by bleeding from the nose, headache, dizziness, bitter taste in the mouth, dryness of throat, redness of eyes, tinnitus, irritability, red tongue with yellow coating and wiry and rapid pulse. 4) Deficiency of *qi* and blood manifested by bleeding of pink blood from the nose or bleeding from the gum, hemathidrosis, fatigue, dizziness, palpitations, pale complexion, restlessness at night, pale tongue and thready and weak pulse.

Pig Skin and Chinese Jujube Thick Soup
Ingredients: Pig's skin 500g
Chinese jujube 250g
Crystal sugar, desired amount
Process: Remove the bristles from the pig's skin. Wash, and put in water. Stew until the soup becomes thick. Add the Chinese jujubes, and cook until they are done, Add crystal sugar to taste.
Usage: This will suffice for several portions eaten at meals.
Indications: Platelet deficiency, nose-bleeding in hemophiliacs, bleeding gums.
Source: *Folk Effective Recipes*

Water Spinach Soup
Ingredients: Water spinach 500g
Crystal sugar (or honey) 50g
Process: Wash the water spinach, and cut into pieces. Add water, and boil until the vegetable is tender. Remove the vegetable, and reduce the soup until there is one rice bowl left. Add the crystal sugar or honey. Cool to room temperature before drinking.
Usage: Take twice daily.
Indications: Nose bleeding, and blood in the urine and stool.
Source: *Notes on Herb Collection in Lingnan Region*

Sugar and Egg White Thick Soup
Ingredients: Egg white 50g
Sugar 50g
Process: Mix together the chicken egg white and the sugar. Stir in boiling water to cook the eggs.
Usage: Cool to lukewarm, and serve, twice daily.
Indications: Childhood nose bleeding.
Source: *Chinese Medicated Diet*

6.2.21 Blood in the Urine
Blood in the urine can be classified as: 1) Accumulation of heat in lower *jiao* manifested by hot feeling during urination with discharge of bright red blood, restlessness, thirst, flushed face, palpitation,

sleeplessness, red tongue and rapid pulse. 2) Hyperactivity of fore and deficiency of kidneys manifested by oliguria, hematuria, dizziness, tinnitus, spiritlessness, thinness, flushed cheeks, hectic fever, soreness and weakness of loins and knees, red tongue and thready and rapid pulse. 3) Failure of controlling blood by the spleen manifested by long-term hematuria with discharge of reddish urine, lusterless complexion, fatigue, shortness of breath, poor appetite, bleeding from gum, epistaxis, hemathidrosis, corpulent pale tongue and thready and weak pulse. 4) Deficiency of kidney-*qi* manifested by long-term hematuria with discharge of reddish urine, frequent urination, nocturia, dizziness, tinnitus, spiritlessness, lumbago, pale tongue and deep and weak pulse.

The Base of Lotus Leaf Soup

Ingredients: The base of lotus leaves, 5 pieces

Crystal sugar, a little

Process: Use the base of five lotus leaves, the center part where it meets the stem, but do not use the stem itself. Wash, and cut into pieces. Cook in some water for one hour. Use only the soup portion, mixing with a little crystal sugar.

Usage: Drink warm, two or three times per day.

Indications: Blood in the urine or stool.

Source: *Prescriptions for Caring All People*

Bamboo and Woolly Grass Drink

Ingredients: Bamboo leaves 10g

Woolly grass 10g

Process: Place the bamboo leaves and woolly grass in a thermos. Pour in boiling water, cover tightly, and steep for half an hour.

Usage: Drink as tea.

Indications: Blood in the urine.

Source: *Herbal Medicines in Jiangxi Province*

Lotus and Rice Cake

Ingredients: Lotus root flour 250g

Glutinous rice flour 250g

Sugar 250g

Process: Mix the lotus root flour, glutinous rice flour and sugar together with water to form a dough. Place on a steamer rack and steam until done.

Usage: Eat in any amount, either boiled or pan-fried.

Indications: This cake will nourish the stomach, fortify weakness, and stop bleeding. Eaten continuously, it will be good for the patients who suffered from debility, poor appetite, nose bleeding, spitting of blood, and blood in the urine or stool.

Source: *A Supplement to the Great Herbalism*

6.2.22 Debility and Emaciation

Debility and emaciation includes various chronic debilitation disorders in which the deficiency of *zang-fu* organs and the insufficiency of *qi*, blood, *yin* and *yang* constitute its basic pathogenesis. The classification of debility and emaciation is as following:

1) Q*i* deficiency including deficiency of lung-*qi*; deficiency of spleen-*qi*.

2) Blood deficiency including deficiency of heart-blood; deficiency of liver-blood.

3) *Yin* deficiency including deficiency of lung-*yin*; deficiency of heart-*yin*; deficiency of spleen-*yin* and stomach-*yin*; deficiency of liver-*yin*; deficiency of kidney-*yin*.

4) *Yang* deficiency including deficiency of heart-*yang*; deficiency of spleen-*yang*; deficiency of kidney-*yang*.

Radix Ginseng Lotus Soup

Ingredients: Lotus seeds, 10 pieces
White ginseng 10g
Crystal sugar 30g

Process: Remove the pith from the lotus seeds. Put in a pot with the white ginseng. Reconstitute in some water. Add the crystal sugar, and steam in a steamer for one hour. Drink the soup and eat the lotus seeds. Reuse the ginseng with more lotus seeds, steaming in the same manner as before.

Usage: The ginseng can be used three times, and then eaten.

Indications: Debility after illness, emaciation due to deficiency of the spleen, fatigue, spontaneous sweating, and diarrhea.

Source: *Effective Prescriptions*

Dried Longan Sweet Spirit

Ingredients: Dried longan pulp 200g

171

60 percent alcohol clear spirits 400ml

Process: Wash the dried longan pulp and put in a narrow-necked bottle. Add the alcohol clear spirits, and seal, shake once daily for half a month.

Usage: Take 10-20ml twice daily.

Indications: This will warm and fortify the heart and spleen, and aid the nerves, and may be used for weakness and debility, insomnia, amnesia and fear palpitations.

Source: *Wan's Prescriptions*

Fat, Spirits and Chinese Jujube

Ingredients: Chinese jujube 250g
  Mutton fat 25g
  Rice wine 250ml

Process: Boil the Chinese jujubes until they are soft. Drain, and add the mutton fat, and the rice wine. Bring to a boil, and pour into bottle or jar. Seal and store for seven days.

Usage: Eat 3-5 dates twice daily.

Indications: This will strengthen the spleen. It will help debility after illness, lack of heat, and frequent dry mouth.

Source: *Essentially Treasured Prescriptions for Emergencies*

Sweet milk Porridge

Ingredients: Soy bean milk 500ml
  Rice, desired amount
  Sugar, a little

Process: Add the rice to the freshly made soya bean milk. Cook into a porridge, and flavor with a little sugar.

Usage: Eat daily.

Indications: Debility and emaciation, prolonged cough, and dry stool.

Source: *A Supplement to the Great Herbalism*

Malt Sugar Chicken

Ingredients: Chicken 1,000g
  Radix Rehmanniae 30g
  Scallions, a little
  Ginger, a little
  Salt, a little
  Malt sugar 100g

Process: Pluck and eviscerate one chicken and clean it. Stuff the chicken with Radix Rehmanniae, scallions, ginger and a little salt. Then fill with the malt sugar, and sew up the opening. Place the chicken back up in a pot, add some water and cook over small flame until tender.
Usage: To be taken once a day for five days.
Indications: This dish will strengthen weakness and nourish *yin*. It is good for physical weakness due to long illness, emaciation, deficiency of heat and night sweating.
Source: *Yao Zengtan's Collected Effective Prescriptions*

6.2.23 Insomnia

Insomnia has different patterns: difficulty in falling asleep after retiring, early awakening, intermittent waking through the period of attempted sleep, and even inability to sleep all the night. Insomnia is always accompanied by dizziness, headache, palpitation, poor memory or mental disorder.

Jujube Scallion Soup
Ingredients: Chinese jujube, 20 pieces
             Scallions, 7 stalks
Process: Clean the small Chinese jujubes, and reconstitute with water. Cook for 20 minutes, then add the clean scallions (white part and leaves). Continue cooking over low heat for 10 minutes.
Usage: Eat the Chinese jujube and drink the soup.
Indications: Neurosis, weakness after illness, frustration, and insomnia.
Source: *Essentially Treasured Prescriptions for Emergencies*

Ginseng Spirit
Ingredients: White ginseng root 50g
             60% alcohol clear spirits 500ml
Process: Cut the fine white ginseng root, and put in a narrow-necked bottle. Add the 60% alcohol clear spirits. Seal the mouth, and shake once daily. It is ready for use after half a month. As it is consumed, replace about 500ml of the alcohol.
Usage: Take 10-30ml every day at supper.
Indications: Depression, insomnia, fatigue, palpitations, shortness of breath and impotence.
Source: *Folk Effective Recipes*

Chinese Yam, Milk and Mutton Thick Soup

Ingredients: Mutton 500g
Ginger 25g
Fresh Chinese yam 100g
Milk 250ml
Salt, a little

Process: Wash one large chunk of mutton. Stew with the ginger for half a day. Remove one bowl of the mutton soup. Add the peeled and washed fresh Chinese yam. Cook until the yams are tender. Add the cow's milk, and a little salt. Bring to the boil.

Usage: To be taken once a day.

Indications: Eat often, this will help counter physical debility and exhaustion. It is good for cold limbs, cold sweating, fatigue, short of breath, dry mouth, agitated fever, and insomnia, after illness or giving birth.

Source: *Imperial Meals in the Qing Dynasty*

Bitter Bamboo Instant

Ingredients: Fresh bitter bamboo leaves 500g (or dried leaves 250g)
Sugar 250g

Process: Wash the fresh bitter bamboo leaves. Cut into pieces. Cook for one hour, remove the sediments, and continue cooking until the liquid is reduced and thick, and the pot is almost dried. Remove from heat, cool, and add the sugar to absorb all the liquid. Mix, dry, break into pieces, and store in a jar.

Usage: For each use, dissolve 10g in boiling water. Take twice daily.

Indications: Thirst, agitation, and insomnia due to heat diseases.

Source: *General Collection for Holy Relief*

Mutton Heart Roasted with Rose Petals

Ingredients: Fresh rose petals 50g (or dried rose petals 15g)
Mutton heart 500g
Salt, a little

Process: Place the fresh rose petals in a small pot, add salt, and boil in water for 10 minutes and cool. Clean the mutton hearts, cut into chunks, and put chunks on steel or bamboo skewers. Dip the meat into the rose petal-salt mixture, and grill over a flame until tender.

Usage: Eat while hot.

Indications: This will fortify the heart and soothe the spirit. It is good for deficiency of the heart and blood, agitation, and insomnia, and general depression.

Source: *Orthodox Essentials of Dietetics*

6.2.24 Seminal Emission

Seminal emission may be divided into two types: nocturnal emission and spermatorrhea. Generally, in adult males, unmarried or married, occasional emission is not pathological.

a) Nocturnal emission

Nocturnal emission is mainly due to over contemplation or excessive sexual activities which lead to disharmony between the heart and kidney. If the heart fire fails to descend and control the kidney water, the kidney water cannot ascend and cool the heart fire. When water deficiency and fire excess disturb the essence, nocturnal emission happens in dreams. Moreover, there are dizziness, palpitation, listlessness, lassitude and scanty yellow urine, red tongue, and thread, rapid pulse.

b) Spermatorrhea

Spermatorrhea is usually due to damage of the kidney after a prolonged illness, indulgent sexual activity, or stubborn nocturnal emission. In exhaustion of the kidney essence, the loss of *yin* affects *yang*. The primary *qi* of the kidney becomes insufficient, the storage of essence fails and seminal fluid is discharged involuntarily. Clinical manifestations are frequent spermatorrhea during the day or night, particularly if there is a desire for sex, pallor, lassitude, listlessness, pale tongue, and deep, thread, weak pulse.

Fried Chinese Chives with Walnuts

Ingredients: Walnuts 50g
　　　　　　　Chinese chives, desired amount
　　　　　　　Sesame oil, desired amount
　　　　　　　Salt, a little

Process: First, deep fry the walnuts in sesame oil until turning to golden, then cook with Chinese chives that have been cleaned and cut. Flavor with table salt.

Usage: Eat with rice in any amount.
Indications: This will invigorate the kidneys and fortify the *yang*. It will help patients with impotence.
Source: *Oxthodox Formulations & Pulses*

Chinese Yam Rice Balls

Ingredients: Fresh Chinese yam 150g
           Sugar 150g
           Black pepper, a little
           Rice 250g
Process: Steam the washed fresh Chinese yam. Remove the skin, and place in a bowl. Add the sugar, a little black pepper, then mix and mash with a spoon to form filling. Grind the rice into flour, mix with some water, and make a dough. Wrap the filling with rice dough to make little round dumplings. Boil the rice balls before eating.
Usage: To be taken once a day.
Indications: This will fortify the kidneys and nourish *yin*. Eaten often, it will cure weak semen and infertility in men due to weakness or cold in the kidneys.
Source: *Liu Changchun's Case Records and Prescriptions*

Steamed Chinese Yam

Ingredients: Fresh Chinese yam 500g
           Flour 150g
           Walnut meats, desired amount
           Various kinds of fruits, desired amount
           Honey syrup, one tablespoon
           Sugar 100g
           Starch, a little
Process: Wash the fresh Chinese yam. Steam until done, remove the skin, and place in a large bowl. Add the flour. Mix the yam and flour and make a dough. Roll the dough out into a shape, and place on a plate. On top of the dough, arrange walnut meats and various kinds of fruits. Steam for 20 minutes. Finally, glaze the cake with honey syrup (honey syrup is made by cooking together one tablespoon of honey, sugar, lard and a little starch). This cake is pretty, tasty and refreshing.
Usage: To be taken once a day.

Indications: It will nourish the kidneys and *yang*. Eaten often, it will be very beneficial to nutrition. It is good for debility due to deficiency of the kidneys, excessive thirst, frequent urination, and seminal emission.
Source: *Folk Cookbook*

6.2.25 Goiter

Goiter is an enlargement of the thyroid gland, which causes a swelling in the front part of the neck. It can be classified as stagnation of *qi* and retention of phlegm; accumulation of phlegm and blood stasis; hyperactivity of liver-fire; deficiency of the liver-*yin* and heart-*yin* according to the theory of TCM.

Green Persimmon Juice Syrup
Ingredients: Unripe green persimmons 1,000g
            Honey, desired amount
Process: Pick and wash the unripe green persimmons. Remove the stems and cut and mash. Squeeze the juice out through a clean cloth. Place the juice in a pot, and cook over high heat, then reduce the heat, and simmer until thick. Add twice as much honey as there is liquid in the pot. Continue to cook until thick and syrupy. Remove from heat, cool, and store in a jar.
Usage: Twice daily, dissolve one tablespoonful in boiling water, and drink.
Indications: Goiter due to geographical location, or hyperthyroidism, as the case may be.
Source: *Folk Effective Recipes*

Seaweed and Radish Soup
Ingredients: White radish 250g
            Seaweed, 15g
            Orange peel, two small pieces
            Salt, a little
Process: Wash and shred the white radish. Slice the seaweed and the orange peel. Place in a pot, and some water, and cook for half an hour. Before taking out of the pot, flavor with salt or other spices.
Usage: Eat the radish and seaweed, and drink the soup twice daily.
Indications: Goiter and lymphatic tuberculosis.
Source: *Folk Effective Recipes*

Kelp Powder

Ingredients: Kelp 500g
Seaweed 500g
Process: Bake kelp and seaweed until dry. Grind into powder and take 10g daily. 250g may also be made into soup.
Usage: Take 10g daily. Take daily for half a month.
Indications: Simple goiter.
Source: *Eating Your Way to Health*

6.2.26   Menstrual Disorder

Menstrual disorder refers to abnormal changes in menstrual cycle, intermenstrual period, menstrual flow, color of menses and nature of menses. In TCM it is believed that menstrual disorder is mainly related to excess or deficiency of *qi* and blood as well as functions of viscera and is classified into preceded menstrual cycle, delayed menstrual cycle, irregular menstrual cycle, menorrhagia, oligomenorrhea and so on.

An Edible Fungus Candy

Ingredients: Brown sugar 500g
Powdered an edible fungus 200g
Process: Put the brown sugar in a pot and add some water. Cook over low flame until it becomes syrupy, then add the finely powdered edible fungus. Mix well, then remove from heat. Pour on to a greased plate and cool. Press it flat and cut into small pieces. After cooling, the candy will be a brownish-black sugary slab.
Usage: To be taken as desired.
Indications: It will stop bleeding. Frequent consumption will help excessive menstruation and uterine bleeding.
Source: *Folk Effective Recipes*

Quick-Boiled Oysters

Ingredients: Fresh shucked oysters 250g
Salt, a little
MSG, a little
Process: Bring some chicken broth or other clear soup made from lean meat to a rolling boil. Quickly drop the fresh shucked oysters in the soup, and bring to a boil again. Spice with salt and MSG.
Usage: Eat the oysters and drink the soup.

Indications: This dish nourishes *yin* and blood. It is good for weakness in a long illness, excessive menstrual flow, uterine bleeding, and erysipelas.
Source: *A Supplement to the Great Herbalism*

Sesame Oil Syrup
Ingredients: Sesame oil 100g
Honey 200g
Process: Separately bring the sesame oil and the honey to the boil over a low flame. Remove from heat, and cool to lukewarm. Mix with the sesame oil and honey.
Usage: Eat one tablespoonful directly, twice daily.
Indications: Bleeding from threatened or spontaneous abortion.
Source: *Instructions for Better Delivery*

6.2.27 Insufficient Lactation

Insufficient lactation refers to the common clinical symptom that milk secretion of a nursing mother is insufficient to feed the baby. In some cases there may be no secretion of milk at all. Ancient people named it as lack of milk and halted milk flow due to deficiency of *qi* and blood or to stagnation of the liver-*qi*. It is clinically classified into deficiency and excess types (deficiency of *qi* and blood, liver-*qi* stagnation).

Fresh Lettuce Root Salad
Ingredients: Fresh Lettuce root 250g
Salt, a little
Rice wine, a little
Process: Wash and peel lettuce root. Cut into thin strips and mix well with salt and rice wine to taste.
Usage: To be taken once a day.
Indications: This will help letting down milk, and is a diuretic. It is especially recommended for inability to pass milk or urinate after giving birth.
Source: *Overseas Prescriptions*

Black Sesame Porridge
Ingredients: Black sesame seed 25g

Rice, desired amount

Process: Crush fine black sesame seeds. Wash any amount of rice desired, and boil it in water with black sesame seeds until thick. Take often at meals.

Usage: To be taken once a day.

Indications: It will strengthen the liver and kidneys, and moisten the Five Viscera. It is suitable for dizziness and weakness in old age, emaciation, dry stools, premature graying of hair, and scanty mother's milk.

Source: *Compendium of Materia Medica*

Pig Trotters and Peanuts

Ingredients: Pig's trotters two pieces

Peanuts 200g

Salt, a little

Process: Wash and score two pig's trotters. Place in pot with the peanuts and some salt to taste. Boil in water over low flame until tender, and meat can slip from the bones.

Usage: Eat at each separate meal, taking the meat and drinking the soup.

Indications: This will nourish the blood and fortify *yin* and aids in letting down milk. It is good for scanty milk or its stoppage.

Source: *Lu Chuan Herbalism*

Black Sesame Salt

Ingredients: Black sesame seeds 50g

Salt 25g

Process: Put the black sesame seeds and the salt in a pot and dry-fry until the sesame is cooked. When cooled, crush the mixture into a fine powder.

Usage: This can be used as a filling or as a dip.

Indications: It will alleviate debility and assist in letting down milk. It is good when there is little or no mother's milk.

Source: *Compendium of Materia Medica*

6.2.28 Pediatric Diseases and Syndromes

There are many pediatric diseases and syndromes which are suitable to treat with functional food. Here, we just introduce three functional foods for some common syndromes, for instance, abdominal pain, and diarrhea due to stomach and intestinal flu, whooping cough and emaciation due to infantile malnutrition and so on.

Cucumber Leaf Instant

Ingredients: Fresh cucumber leaves 1,000g
　　　　　　 Sugar 500g

Process: Wash the fresh cucumber leaves. Add to some water, and cook for one hour. Remove the sediments. Continue to cook over low heat until reduced and almost dry. Remove from heat, and cool. Mix in the sugar. Dry in the sun, then break into pieces and store in a jar.

Usage: Dissolve 10g in some boiling water for each dose. Take three times daily.

Indications: Fever, abdominal pain, and diarrhea due to stomach and intestinal flu in children.

Source: *Herbal Medicines in Chongqing Region*

Duck Egg and Crystal Sugar Thick Soup

Ingredients: Duck eggs, two
　　　　　　 Crystal sugar 50g

Process: Dissolve the crystal sugar in some hot water. Cool, and add two duck eggs. Mix and beat, then steam until done.

Usage: This can serve as one dose or many, to be eaten once a day.

Indications: Whooping cough.

Source: *Chinese Medicated Diet*

Clove and Ginger in Milk

Ingredients: Cloves, two pieces
　　　　　　 Ginger juice, one teaspoon
　　　　　　 Cow's milk 250ml
　　　　　　 Sugar, a little

Process: Put the cloves, ginger juice and the cow's milk in a pot, and bring to the boil. Remove the cloves and add a little sugar.

Usage: To be taken once a day.

Indications: This will strengthen and fortify, lessen the flow of vital energy, and stop nausea. It is suitable for emaciation due to infantile malnutrition because of a digestive disturbance or intestinal parasites, and can be taken by children who are feeling too nauseous to eat.

Source: *Simple Prescriptions for Health*

6.2.29   Congestion, Swelling and Pain of the Eye

Congestion, swelling and pain of the eye are acute conditions in various external eye disorders.

This conditions are mostly due to exogenous pathogenic wind heat causing obstruction of *qi* circulation in the meridians, or due to preponderance of fire in the liver and gallbladder which flares up along the related meridians causing *qi* stagnation and blood stasis in the meridians.

Bitter Melon in Lard

Ingredients: Bitter melon 250g
　　　　　　Lard, a little
　　　　　　Scallions, a little
　　　　　　Ginger, a little
　　　　　　Salt, a little

Process: Wash the bitter melon, remove seeds. Cook quickly in lard, flavor with scallions and ginger, a little salt, and serve with rice.

Usage: To be taken once a day.

Indications: This will relieve heat, nourish the liver, clear the eyes, lubricate the liver, and invigorate the kidneys. It is good for the patients with weak or hot eye trouble, weak spleen, and physical debility.

Source: *Cookbook for Food & Drinks in Daily Life*

Watermelon Instant

Ingredients: Watermelon, one
　　　　　　Sugar, desired amount

Process: Remove the seeds from watermelon flesh. Squeeze the juice out with a clean cloth. Cook first over high heat then over low heat until the watermelon juice becomes thick and syrupy. Remove from heat and cool. Add enough sugar to absorb the liquid, mix, and dry in the sun. Break into small pieces, and store in a jar.

Usage: For each dose, dissolve 15g in boiling water, and drink 3 times daily.

Indications: Edema, thirst due to heat disease or diabetes, and red, swollen eyes.

Source: *Travels in Songmo*

Chicken Liver Thick Soup

Ingredients: Chicken's livers 50g

Salt, a little

Process: Wash chicken's livers. Remove membranes, and cut into slices. Quick-boil the livers by dumping them in rolling boiling water. They are done when they change color and are no longer bloody.

Usage: Eat the soup while hot, flavoring with a little salt or other seasoning.

Indications: Poor vision and night blindness due to malnutrition.

Source: *New Book for Old People and Longevity*

Pig's Liver Soup

Ingredients: Pig's liver 100g
Fermented black beans, desired amount
The white part of scallions, a little
An egg

Process: Wash the pork liver. Remove the sinews and membranes, and slice the liver. Put in water, and cook over low heat. When the liver is done, add some fermented black beans, and the white part of scallions, then poach an egg in the soup.

Usage: Drink the soup and eat the liver and the egg.

Indications: Weak vision, far-sightedness, and night blindness.

Source: *Imperial Benevolent Prescriptions of the Taiping Period*

Sheep's Liver in Soy Sauce and Vinegar

Ingredients: Sheep's liver 500g
Vegetable oil, a little
Soy sauce, a little
Vinegar, a little
Sugar, a little
Rice wine, a little
Fresh ginger, a little
Scallions, a little

Process: Clean the sheep's liver, slice and coat with starch solution, heat some vegetable oil in a pan and stir fry quickly. Add soy sauce, vinegar, sugar, rice wine, ginger and scallions. When the sheep's liver is tender and cooked, it is done.

Usage: To be taken once a day.

Indications: This dish will nourish the liver and clear the eyes. Eaten often, it will cure insufficiency of the liver and physical debility, weakness of vision, and night blindness.

6.2.30   Sore Throat

Sore throat is commonly seen. It can be divided into two types: excess and deficiency.

The throat communicates with the stomach and the lung through the esophagus and the trachea respectively. Sore throat of excess type (excess of heat) is due to exogenous pathogenic wind heat that scorches the lung system or due to the accumulated heat in the lung and stomach meridians that disturbs upward. Sore throat of deficiency type (deficiency of *yin*) is due to the exhaustion of the kidney *yin* that fails to flow upward to moisten the throat, while the asthenia fire flares up instead.

Water Chestnut Juice

Ingredients: Fresh water chestnuts 1,000g
Crystal sugar, a little
Process: Wash the fresh water chestnuts, peel, and cut into pieces. Squeeze them through a clean cloth.
Usage: This may be taken cold in any quantity. Some crystal sugar may be added if desired.
Indications: It will alleviate acute and chronic infections of the throat.
Source: *Quanzhou Herbalism*

Sugared Kelp

Ingredients: Kelp 500g
Sugar 250g
Process: Soak and reconstitute the kelp and wash away any salt. Cut into pieces, place in a pot, and add some water. Cook until done, remove from water, and place in a soup dish. Mix in 250g sugar, and marinate for one day.
Usage: Take 50g twice daily.
Indications: This product has softening and dispelling properties. It will cure chronic throat infections.
Source: *Folk Effective Recipes*

Liquorice Root and Radix Platycodi Instant

Ingredients: Liquorice root 60g
Radix Platycodi 30g
Sugar 200g

Process: Use cold water to reconstitute liquorice root, and Radix Platycodi. Add some water and cook. Every 20 minutes, remove the liquid, add more water, and continue cooking. Collect the liquid three times and combine the liquid. Boil the liquid over low heat until it becomes concentrated and thick. Remove from heat and cool. Mix in the dry powdered sugar until the liquid is fully absorbed by the sugar. Dry it and break into small pieces. Store in a jar.

Usage: When used, dissolve 10g in boiling water, and drink often, at least three times a day.

Indications: Chronic and acute pharyngitis and laryngitis.

Source: *Treatises on Febrile and Miscellaneous Diseases*

6.3 For Prevention

6.3.1 The Concept of Prevention with Functional Food

Traditional Chinese medicine has always attached great importance to prevention. *The Emperor's Canon of Medicine* emphasizes "giving treatment before a disease arises." And *Basic Questions* states, "Great practitioners give treatment before diseases occur and prevent disorders before they rise. To give treatment when a disease has occurred is late. This is similar to not digging a well until you are thirsty or not making weapons until the war break out." Giving treatment before a disease arises includes two aspects: disease prevention and the prevention of diseases from deteriorating.

Preventive medicine in ancient China had two aspects - self-care and legislation for public health. Of the two it seems the former was accorded the greatest importance. *The Emperor's Canon of Medicine* pays great attention to the achievement of a good balance both in one's mental and physical states, believing that security and a calm mind were prerequisites of good physical health.

Science is beginning to uncover the role of food and is discovering a physiological role for nutrients beyond deficiency diseases and for other constituents of foods such as antioxidants, bioactive lipids, biopolymers, phytoestrogens, flavors and colors, etc. In fact, the term "functional foods" is being applied to a broad spectrum of foods ranging from conventional or standard foods for nourishment and well-being to foods which have been modified nutritionally in their micronutrient and/or macronutrient contents, to those which have been transformed into foods which contain various amounts of physiologically active components or ingredients conferring recognizable prophylactic or therapeutic effects.

Modern studies will allow us to maximize both the functional properties of ingredients within food to make better more appealing products, as well as to understand their physiological behavior within the body.

In addition to the nutrients necessary for normal metabolic activity, foods contain components that may provide additional health benefits. These food components are derived from naturally occurring ingredients and are being actively investigated for their health-promoting potential. Examples include indoles, isothiocyanates, and sulforaphne, found in vegetables such as broccoli, which have been shown to trigger enzyme systems that block or suppress cellular DNA damage, reduce tumor size (in animals), and decrease the effectiveness of estrogen-like hormones. Allylic sulfides, found in onions and garlic, are another example; they enhance immune function, increase production of enzymes that help excrete carcinogens, decrease the proliferation of tumor cells, and reduce serum cholesterol levels.

In addition, there are "functional foods," which are defined as modified foods or food ingredients that may provide a health benefit beyond that of the traditional nutrients the food contains. Examples here include Vitamin C-enriched oranges, high-phytochemical broccoli, and fiber-enriched baked products. Phytochemicals and functional foods have been associated with the prevention and/or treatment of at least four of the leading causes of death in the United States - cancer, diabetes, cardiovascular disease, and hypertension - and in the prevention and/or treatment of other medical ailments including neural tube defects, osteoporosis, abnormal bowel function, and arthritis. The benefits of phytochemicals and functional foods have been publicized in the popular press, resulting in increased public awareness and interest in consuming phytochemical-rich foods and functional foods as a method of enhancing health and well-being. Although scientific reports of clinical benefits are few, evidence is mounting to support the incorporation of foods rich in phytochemicals into the diets of most Americans. In a position paper on the subject, the American Dietetic Association (ADA) states that phytochemicals and functional food components may both have beneficial roles when consumed as part of a varied diet.

Health benefits linked to these functional foods the importance of incorporating specific foods, such as fruits and vegetables, into our diet becomes really clear.

The benefit could be something that's added, such as extra fiber. Or it could result from something taken away from the food, such as an allergen. Some foods are familiar but have been produced in a different way so that the composition is altered a little. Here are a few familiar examples:

Added Fiber

There are several cereals on the market with extra fibers. The fiber might be added wheat bran, or another kind of fiber such as psyllium. New research is resulting in foods like white bread or buns with barley fiber, or pasta with pea fiber. Since we know that a diet rich in soluble fiber helps to decrease blood levels of cholesterol, foods with added fiber are likely to be very popular.

The concept of prevention with food consists of two aspects:

1) Strengthening the body's constitution and promoting immunity to disease in general through scientific food structure. It means building up health and strengthening resistance to diseases.

2) Preventing certain diseases by elimination of pathogenic factors or supplying specific nutrition, for instance, to prevent diarrhea and cancer with garlic, etc.

One thousand years ago, it was recorded that night blindness could be prevented with animal liver. Goiters could be prevented with kelp. Scurvy could be prevented by eating fruit and vegetable. Modern nutritionists have proved that deficiencies in the diet will cause people to suffer from certain diseases, for instance, night blindness caused by deficiency of Vitamin A; goiter caused by deficiency of iodine; scurvy caused by deficiency of Vitamin C, etc.

The possibilities are endless. Scientists are identifying more and more components of foods which are known to have health benefits. We can expect that food scientists will look for ways to isolate those components and add them to other foods in order to maximize the benefit. It's not a new concept – we've been adding vitamins to milk, margarine, and cereals for decades.

In recent years, some herbs have been used successfully to prevent many diseases. Flu, for example, is prevented with Rhizoma Dryopteris Cassirhizomae, Radix Isatidis or folium Isatidis; hepatitis is prevented with Herba Artemisias Scopariae, Fructus Gardeniae; and dysentery is prevented with Herba Portulacae.

In addition, the modern nutritionists have proved that the soup made from green Chinese onion, fermented soy beans and coriander can be used to prevent colds. Mung bean soup can be used to prevent sunstroke. Chinese hawthorn can prevent indigestion, etc. (See Table 14.)

6.3.2   Common Functional Food for Prevention

Table 14   Common Functional Food for Prevention

Name of functional food	Prevention
Black Carp with Ginger and Green Chinese Onion	cold
Honeyed Cherry with Licorice Root	pharyngitis and laryngitis
Fried Spinach Stems with Egg White	diabetes mellitus
Green Tea and Duck Eggs	diabetes mellitus
Sparrow in Brown Sauce with Pilose Antler of a Young Stag	impotence
Tremella, an Edible Fungus and Mushroom in Gravy	deficiency of *qi* and *yin*
Fried Eel with Eucommia Bark and Dried Rehmannia Root	hypertension
Watermelon and Tomato Juice	summer-heat
Fried Bitter Melon	summer-heat
Fried Fragrant-Flowered Garlic with Walnut	impotence
Ginseng, Shrimp and Winter Melon Soup	lassitude and edema of limbs
Chinese Yam Honeyed Pancake	deficiency of the spleen-*qi*
Corn Silk Drink	edema and lumbago
Mung Bean Soup	summer-heat
Corn Silk and Red Bean Soup	edema
Fresh Vegetable Thick Soup	cancer

Appendix

The Chinese and English Names of the Books Mentioned in This Book

Han Yu Pin Yin	Chinese Character	English Name
Bei Ji Qian Jin Yao Fang	备急千金要方	*One Thousand Precious Prescriptions (Essentially Treasured Prescriptions for Emergencies)*
Ben Cao Gang Mu	本草纲目	*Compendium of Materia Medica (The Great Herbalism)*
Ben Cao Gang Mu Shi Yi	本草纲目拾遗	*A Supplement to the Great Herbalism (A Supplement to Compendium of Materia Media)*
Ben Cao Hui Yan	本草汇言	*Collection of Herbalism*
Ben Cao Qiu Yuan	本草求原	*Probing the Origin of Herbalism*
Ben Cao Zai Xin	本草再新	*Renew Herbalism*
Bian Chan Xu Zhi	便产须知	*Instructions for Better Delivery*
Bian Min Shi Liao	便民食疗	*Food Therapy for Laymen*
Bu Que Zhou Hou Fang	补缺肘后方	*A Supplement to Handbook of Prescriptions for Emergencies*
Chong Qing Cao Yao	重庆草药	*Herbal Medicines in Chongqing Region*
Dian Nan Ben Cao	滇南本草	*Herbalism in Yunnan Province*

Fang Mai Zheng Zong	方脉正宗	*Oxthodox Formulations & Pulses*
Fei Shi Shi Yang	费氏食养	*Fei's Health Preserving with Food*
Fu Jian Zhong Cao Yao	福建中草药	*Chinese Materia Medica in Fujian Province*
Guang Dong Liang Cha Yan Fang	广东凉茶验方	*Effective Recipes of Cold Tea in Guangdong Province*
Hai Shang Fang	海上方	*Overseas Prescriptions*
Huai Nan Zi	淮南子	*A Book About Chinese Culture and History in Han Dynasty*
Huang Di Nei JIng	黄帝内经	*The Emperor's Canon of Medicine (The Inner Canon of the Yellow Emperor)*
Huo Ren Xin Tong	活人心统	*Orthodox for Saving Lives*
Jiang Xi Cao Yao	江西草药	*Herbal Medicines in Jiangxi Province*
Jin Kui Yao Lue	金匮要略	*Synopsis of Prescriptions of the Golden Chamber (Synopsis of the Golden Cabinet)*
Jing Yan Guang Ji	经验广集	*Collection of Experience and Prescriptions*
Jing Yan Liang Fang	经验良方	*Effective Prescriptions*
Jiu Ji Fang	救急方	*Prescriptions for Emergencies*
Ling Nan Cai Yao Lu	岭南采药录	*Notes on Herb Collection in Lingnan Region*
Liu Chang Chun Jing Yan Ji	刘长春经验集	*Liu Changchun's Case Records and Prescriptions*
Lu Chuan Ben Cao	陆川本草	*Lu Chuan Herbalism*
Meng Shen Fang	孟诜方	*Meng Shen's Prescriptions*

Min Jian Shi Pu	民间食谱	*Folk Cookbook*
Min Jian Yan Fang	民间验方	*Folk Effective Recipes*
Pu Ji Fang	普济方	*Prescriptions for Caring All People (Prescriptions of Universal Benevolence)*
Qing Gong Yu Shan Pu	清宫御膳谱	*Imperial Meals in the Qing Dynasty*
Quan Zhou Ben Cao	泉州本草	*Quanzhou Herbalism*
Ren Zhai Zhi Zhi Fang	仁斋直指方	*Ren Zhai's Prescriptions*
Ri Yong Ben Cao	日用本草	*Materia Medica for Daily Use*
Ru Men Shi Qin	儒门事亲	*The Literati's Care of Their Parents*
Shan Jia Qing Gong	山家清供	*Vegetable Meals of Hill Inhabitants*
Shang Han Za Bing Lun	伤寒杂病论	*Treatises on Febrile and Miscellaneous Diseases (Treatises on Cold Diseases and Miscellaneous Disorders)*
Shen Nong Ben Cao Jing	神农本草经	*Shen Nong's Materia Medica (Shen Nong's Classic of Herbalism)*
Sheng Ji Zong Lu	圣济总录	*General Collection for Holy Relief (The Imperial Medical Encyclopedia)*
Shi Liao Ben Cao	食疗本草	*Materia Medica of Food Therapy (Herbalism of Food Therapy)*
Shi Wu Ben Cao Hui Zuan	食物本草会纂	*Compiled of Herbalism of Food*
Shi Wu Mi Shu	食物秘书	*Secret Book of Food*

Shi Yang Fang	补养方	*Nourishing Prescriptions*
Shi Yi Xin Jing	食医心镜	*Reflections of Food Doctors*
Shou Qin Yang Lao Xin Shu	寿亲养老新书	*New Book for Old People and Longevity*
Shuo Wen Jie Zi	说文解字	*A Dictionary of Characters*
Song Mo Ji Xing	松漠纪行	*Travels in Songmo*
Sui Xi Ju Yin Shi Pu	随息居饮食谱	*Cookbook for Food & Drinks in Daily Life*
Sui Yuan Shi Dan	随园食单	*Recipes for Suiyuan*
Tai Ping Sheng Hui Fang	太平圣惠方	*Imperial Benevolent Prescriptions of the Taiping Period*
Tang Ye Jing	汤液经	*The Soup and Decoctions*
Tang Xin Xiu Ben Cao	唐·新修本草	*Newly Compiled Materia Medica of the Tang Dynasty (Newly Revised Herbalism)*
Tiao Ji Yin Shi Bian	调疾饮食辩	*Food Therapy for Common Diseases*
Wan Shi Jia Chao Fang	万氏家抄方	*Wan's Prescriptions*
Wei Sheng Yi Jian Fang	卫生易简方	*Simple Prescriptions for Health*
Wu Shi Er Bing Fang	五十二病方	*Prescriptions for Fifty-Two Kinds of Diseases*
Xu Si Bo Fang	徐嗣伯方	*Xu Sibo's Prescriptions*
Yan Fang	验方	*Effective Recipes*
Yang Lao Feng Qin Shu	养老奉亲书	*Health Care of Parents and Old People*
Yao Zeng Tan Ji Yan Fang	姚增坦集验方	*Yao Zengtan's Collected Effective Prescriptions*
Yi Xue Da Ci Dian	医学大辞典	*Dictionary of Chinese Medicine*

Yi Xue Fa Ming	医学发明	*Invention of Medicine*
Yin Liao 100 Li	饮疗 100 例	*100 Cases of Drink Therapy*
Yin Shan Zheng Yao	饮膳正要	*Essentials of Food and Drink* *(Orthodox Essentials of Dietetics)*
Yin Shi Shi Er He Lun	饮食十二合论	*Twelve Comments on Diet*
Zhong Guo Yao Shan	中国药膳	*Chinese Medicated Diet*
Zhong Guo Yao Wu Zhi	中国药物志	*Collection of Chinese Materia Medica*
Zhou Li	周礼	*The Rites of the Zhou Dynasty*

图书在版编目（ CIP ）数据

中国功能食品/党毅主编．-北京：新世界出版社，1999
ISBN 7-80005-555-8

I. 中 ... II. 党 ... III. 疗效食品-概况-中国
IV. TS218

中国版本图书馆 CIP 数据核字（ 1999 ）第 44083 号

中 国 功 能 食 品

主　　编：党　毅
责任编辑：任玲娟
封面设计：贺玉婷
版式设计：方　维
出版发行：新世界出版社
社　　址：北京阜城门外百万庄路 24 号
邮政编码：100037
电　　话：0086-10-68994118
传　　真：0086-10-68326679
经　　销：中国国际图书贸易总公司发行
印　　刷：北京晨光印刷厂
开　　本：850 × 1168　1/32
字　　数：100 千
印　　张：6.75
版　　次：1999 年 10 月（英）第 1 版第 1 次印刷
书　　号：ISBN 7-80005-555-8/G · 188
定　　价：18.00 元

17E-3356P